C-2440   CAREER EXAMINATION SERIES

This is your
PASSBOOK for...

Signal Electrician

Test Preparation Study Guide
Questions & Answers

NATIONAL LEARNING CORPORATION®

COPYRIGHT NOTICE

This book is SOLELY intended for, is sold ONLY to, and its use is RESTRICTED to individual, bona fide applicants or candidates who qualify by virtue of having seriously filed applications for appropriate license, certificate, professional and/or promotional advancement, higher school matriculation, scholarship, or other legitimate requirements of education and/or governmental authorities.

This book is NOT intended for use, class instruction, tutoring, training, duplication, copying, reprinting, excerption, or adaptation, etc., by:

1) Other publishers
2) Proprietors and/or Instructors of "Coaching" and/or Preparatory Courses
3) Personnel and/or Training Divisions of commercial, industrial, and governmental organizations
4) Schools, colleges, or universities and/or their departments and staffs, including teachers and other personnel
5) Testing Agencies or Bureaus
6) Study groups which seek by the purchase of a single volume to copy and/or duplicate and/or adapt this material for use by the group as a whole without having purchased individual volumes for each of the members of the group
7) Et al.

Such persons would be in violation of appropriate Federal and State statutes.

PROVISION OF LICENSING AGREEMENTS – Recognized educational, commercial, industrial, and governmental institutions and organizations, and others legitimately engaged in educational pursuits, including training, testing, and measurement activities, may address request for a licensing agreement to the copyright owners, who will determine whether, and under what conditions, including fees and charges, the materials in this book may be used them. In other words, a licensing facility exists for the legitimate use of the material in this book on other than an individual basis. However, it is asseverated and affirmed here that the material in this book CANNOT be used without the receipt of the express permission of such a licensing agreement from the Publishers. Inquiries re licensing should be addressed to the company, attention rights and permissions department.

All rights reserved, including the right of reproduction in whole or in part, in any form or by any means, electronic or mechanical, including photocopying, recording, or by any information storage and retrieval system, without permission in writing from the Publisher.

Copyright © 2025 by
National Learning Corporation

212 Michael Drive, Syosset, NY 11791
(516) 921-8888 • www.passbooks.com
E-mail: info@passbooks.com

PASSBOOK® SERIES

THE *PASSBOOK® SERIES* has been created to prepare applicants and candidates for the ultimate academic battlefield – the examination room.

At some time in our lives, each and every one of us may be required to take an examination – for validation, matriculation, admission, qualification, registration, certification, or licensure.

Based on the assumption that every applicant or candidate has met the basic formal educational standards, has taken the required number of courses, and read the necessary texts, the *PASSBOOK® SERIES* furnishes the one special preparation which may assure passing with confidence, instead of failing with insecurity. Examination questions – together with answers – are furnished as the basic vehicle for study so that the mysteries of the examination and its compounding difficulties may be eliminated or diminished by a sure method.

This book is meant to help you pass your examination provided that you qualify and are serious in your objective.

The entire field is reviewed through the huge store of content information which is succinctly presented through a provocative and challenging approach – the question-and-answer method.

A climate of success is established by furnishing the correct answers at the end of each test.

You soon learn to recognize types of questions, forms of questions, and patterns of questioning. You may even begin to anticipate expected outcomes.

You perceive that many questions are repeated or adapted so that you can gain acute insights, which may enable you to score many sure points.

You learn how to confront new questions, or types of questions, and to attack them confidently and work out the correct answers.

You note objectives and emphases, and recognize pitfalls and dangers, so that you may make positive educational adjustments.

Moreover, you are kept fully informed in relation to new concepts, methods, practices, and directions in the field.

You discover that you are actually taking the examination all the time: you are preparing for the examination by "taking" an examination, not by reading extraneous and/or supererogatory textbooks.

In short, this PASSBOOK®, used directedly, should be an important factor in helping you to pass your test.

SIGNAL ELECTRICIAN

DUTIES:
Under general supervision, installs, maintains, and repairs signals and traffic control equipment. Installs, maintains, repairs, and replaces electric fixtures and cabinets related to traffic signals and street lights. Repairs and adjusts circuit breakers, controls and regulators by replacing worn parts and repairing burned out contacts; Orders parts and keeps a record of time and materials used in electrical installations and repairs; May assist the stationary engineer, master electrician, and carpenters in major department work projects; May supervise or lead a group of employees in various work projects and assignments; Operates motor equipment in transporting equipment, tools and parts. Performs data entry using CarteGraph software to document work and maintain information related to traffic signals, street lights, and other electric components worked on; plans maintenance and capital projects for the street lighting and traffic signal systems.

EXAMPLES OF TYPICAL WORK:
Installs electronic traffic controls and auxiliary equipment; maintains and repairs traffic light fixtures, relays, and controllers; installs and repairs underground and overhead wires and cables; maintains equipment at the signal station; installs and repairs distribution panels; performs a variety of electrical repair tasks; assembles electronic devices and equipment's; assists in training of electrician aides or other helpers; assists in determining the qualifications of products by testing.

SCOPE OF THE EXAMINATION:
The multiple-choice written test will cover knowledge, skills and/or abilities in such areas as:
1. **Basic principles of electricity** - These questions test for knowledge of basic electrical principles including such areas as electric circuit wiring, grounding and insulation; relationships between voltage, current, and resistance in electrical circuits; characteristics of direct current and alternating current circuits; and properties of series and parallel electrical circuits.
2. **Principles, practices, tools and equipment of the electrical trade** - These questions test for knowledge of the principles and practices of the electrical trade, including such areas as tools and equipment used, proper electrical circuit wiring procedures, and appropriate methods of providing safe, efficient, and effective electrical service.
3. **Operation, maintenance and repair of traffic signals and electrical control equipment** - These questions test for knowledge of the principles and practices involved in the operation, maintenance, and repair of various types of traffic signals and related electrical control equipment; and may include such areas as the physical characteristics of traffic signals; proper electronic sequencing, control, and operation of traffic signals; operation of traffic detector circuits; and application of the standards of the State Manual of Uniform Traffic Control Devices to traffic signals.
4. **Basic electronics, including circuitry, schematics, wiring diagrams and tools and test equipment used in electronic repair** - These questions test for knowledge of the concepts, principles, and practices involved in basic electronics, including circuitry, schematics, and wiring diagrams, and the tools and equipment used in the repair of electronic equipment; and may include such areas as the concepts of voltage, current, and resistance; the identification and function of circuit and solid state components; the ability to interpret electronic schematics and wiring diagrams; and identification of the appropriate tools, test equipment, and procedures to use in troubleshooting, maintaining, and repairing electronic equipment.

HOW TO TAKE A TEST

I. YOU MUST PASS AN EXAMINATION

A. WHAT EVERY CANDIDATE SHOULD KNOW

Examination applicants often ask us for help in preparing for the written test. What can I study in advance? What kinds of questions will be asked? How will the test be given? How will the papers be graded?

As an applicant for a civil service examination, you may be wondering about some of these things. Our purpose here is to suggest effective methods of advance study and to describe civil service examinations.

Your chances for success on this examination can be increased if you know how to prepare. Those "pre-examination jitters" can be reduced if you know what to expect. You can even experience an adventure in good citizenship if you know why civil service exams are given.

B. WHY ARE CIVIL SERVICE EXAMINATIONS GIVEN?

Civil service examinations are important to you in two ways. As a citizen, you want public jobs filled by employees who know how to do their work. As a job seeker, you want a fair chance to compete for that job on an equal footing with other candidates. The best-known means of accomplishing this two-fold goal is the competitive examination.

Exams are widely publicized throughout the nation. They may be administered for jobs in federal, state, city, municipal, town or village governments or agencies.

Any citizen may apply, with some limitations, such as the age or residence of applicants. Your experience and education may be reviewed to see whether you meet the requirements for the particular examination. When these requirements exist, they are reasonable and applied consistently to all applicants. Thus, a competitive examination may cause you some uneasiness now, but it is your privilege and safeguard.

C. HOW ARE CIVIL SERVICE EXAMS DEVELOPED?

Examinations are carefully written by trained technicians who are specialists in the field known as "psychological measurement," in consultation with recognized authorities in the field of work that the test will cover. These experts recommend the subject matter areas or skills to be tested; only those knowledges or skills important to your success on the job are included. The most reliable books and source materials available are used as references. Together, the experts and technicians judge the difficulty level of the questions.

Test technicians know how to phrase questions so that the problem is clearly stated. Their ethics do not permit "trick" or "catch" questions. Questions may have been tried out on sample groups, or subjected to statistical analysis, to determine their usefulness.

Written tests are often used in combination with performance tests, ratings of training and experience, and oral interviews. All of these measures combine to form the best-known means of finding the right person for the right job.

II. HOW TO PASS THE WRITTEN TEST

A. NATURE OF THE EXAMINATION

To prepare intelligently for civil service examinations, you should know how they differ from school examinations you have taken. In school you were assigned certain definite pages to read or subjects to cover. The examination questions were quite detailed and usually emphasized memory. Civil service exams, on the other hand, try to discover your present ability to perform the duties of a position, plus your potentiality to learn these duties. In other words, a civil service exam attempts to predict how successful you will be. Questions cover such a broad area that they cannot be as minute and detailed as school exam questions.

In the public service similar kinds of work, or positions, are grouped together in one "class." This process is known as *position-classification*. All the positions in a class are paid according to the salary range for that class. One class title covers all of these positions, and they are all tested by the same examination.

B. FOUR BASIC STEPS

1) Study the announcement

How, then, can you know what subjects to study? Our best answer is: "Learn as much as possible about the class of positions for which you've applied." The exam will test the knowledge, skills and abilities needed to do the work.

Your most valuable source of information about the position you want is the official exam announcement. This announcement lists the training and experience qualifications. Check these standards and apply only if you come reasonably close to meeting them.

The brief description of the position in the examination announcement offers some clues to the subjects which will be tested. Think about the job itself. Review the duties in your mind. Can you perform them, or are there some in which you are rusty? Fill in the blank spots in your preparation.

Many jurisdictions preview the written test in the exam announcement by including a section called "Knowledge and Abilities Required," "Scope of the Examination," or some similar heading. Here you will find out specifically what fields will be tested.

2) Review your own background

Once you learn in general what the position is all about, and what you need to know to do the work, ask yourself which subjects you already know fairly well and which need improvement. You may wonder whether to concentrate on improving your strong areas or on building some background in your fields of weakness. When the announcement has specified "some knowledge" or "considerable knowledge," or has used adjectives like "beginning principles of..." or "advanced ... methods," you can get a clue as to the number and difficulty of questions to be asked in any given field. More questions, and hence broader coverage, would be included for those subjects which are more important in the work. Now weigh your strengths and weaknesses against the job requirements and prepare accordingly.

3) Determine the level of the position

Another way to tell how intensively you should prepare is to understand the level of the job for which you are applying. Is it the entering level? In other words, is this the position in which beginners in a field of work are hired? Or is it an intermediate or advanced level? Sometimes this is indicated by such words as "Junior" or "Senior" in the class title. Other jurisdictions use Roman numerals to designate the level – Clerk I, Clerk II, for example. The word "Supervisor" sometimes appears in the title. If the level is not indicated by the title, check the description of duties. Will you be working under very close supervision, or will you have responsibility for independent decisions in this work?

4) Choose appropriate study materials

Now that you know the subjects to be examined and the relative amount of each subject to be covered, you can choose suitable study materials. For beginning level jobs, or even advanced ones, if you have a pronounced weakness in some aspect of your training, read a modern, standard textbook in that field. Be sure it is up to date and has general coverage. Such books are normally available at your library, and the librarian will be glad to help you locate one. For entry-level positions, questions of appropriate difficulty are chosen – neither highly advanced questions, nor those too simple. Such questions require careful thought but not advanced training.

If the position for which you are applying is technical or advanced, you will read more advanced, specialized material. If you are already familiar with the basic principles of your field, elementary textbooks would waste your time. Concentrate on advanced textbooks and technical periodicals. Think through the concepts and review difficult problems in your field.

These are all general sources. You can get more ideas on your own initiative, following these leads. For example, training manuals and publications of the government agency which employs workers in your field can be useful, particularly for technical and professional positions. A letter or visit to the government department involved may result in more specific study suggestions, and certainly will provide you with a more definite idea of the exact nature of the position you are seeking.

III. KINDS OF TESTS

Tests are used for purposes other than measuring knowledge and ability to perform specified duties. For some positions, it is equally important to test ability to make adjustments to new situations or to profit from training. In others, basic mental abilities not dependent on information are essential. Questions which test these things may not appear as pertinent to the duties of the position as those which test for knowledge and information. Yet they are often highly important parts of a fair examination. For very general questions, it is almost impossible to help you direct your study efforts. What we can do is to point out some of the more common of these general abilities needed in public service positions and describe some typical questions.

1) General information

Broad, general information has been found useful for predicting job success in some kinds of work. This is tested in a variety of ways, from vocabulary lists to questions about current events. Basic background in some field of work, such as sociology or economics, may be sampled in a group of questions. Often these are principles which have become familiar to most persons through exposure rather than through formal training. It is difficult to advise you how to study for these questions; being alert to the world around you is our best suggestion.

2) Verbal ability

An example of an ability needed in many positions is verbal or language ability. Verbal ability is, in brief, the ability to use and understand words. Vocabulary and grammar tests are typical measures of this ability. Reading comprehension or paragraph interpretation questions are common in many kinds of civil service tests. You are given a paragraph of written material and asked to find its central meaning.

3) Numerical ability

Number skills can be tested by the familiar arithmetic problem, by checking paired lists of numbers to see which are alike and which are different, or by interpreting charts and graphs. In the latter test, a graph may be printed in the test booklet which you are asked to use as the basis for answering questions.

4) Observation

A popular test for law-enforcement positions is the observation test. A picture is shown to you for several minutes, then taken away. Questions about the picture test your ability to observe both details and larger elements.

5) Following directions

In many positions in the public service, the employee must be able to carry out written instructions dependably and accurately. You may be given a chart with several columns, each column listing a variety of information. The questions require you to carry out directions involving the information given in the chart.

6) Skills and aptitudes

Performance tests effectively measure some manual skills and aptitudes. When the skill is one in which you are trained, such as typing or shorthand, you can practice. These tests are often very much like those given in business school or high school courses. For many of the other skills and aptitudes, however, no short-time preparation can be made. Skills and abilities natural to you or that you have developed throughout your lifetime are being tested.

Many of the general questions just described provide all the data needed to answer the questions and ask you to use your reasoning ability to find the answers. Your best preparation for these tests, as well as for tests of facts and ideas, is to be at your physical and mental best. You, no doubt, have your own methods of getting into an exam-taking mood and keeping "in shape." The next section lists some ideas on this subject.

IV. KINDS OF QUESTIONS

Only rarely is the "essay" question, which you answer in narrative form, used in civil service tests. Civil service tests are usually of the short-answer type. Full instructions for answering these questions will be given to you at the examination. But in case this is your first experience with short-answer questions and separate answer sheets, here is what you need to know:

1) Multiple-choice Questions

Most popular of the short-answer questions is the "multiple choice" or "best answer" question. It can be used, for example, to test for factual knowledge, ability to solve problems or judgment in meeting situations found at work.

A multiple-choice question is normally one of three types—
- It can begin with an incomplete statement followed by several possible endings. You are to find the one ending which *best* completes the statement, although some of the others may not be entirely wrong.
- It can also be a complete statement in the form of a question which is answered by choosing one of the statements listed.

- It can be in the form of a problem – again you select the best answer.

Here is an example of a multiple-choice question with a discussion which should give you some clues as to the method for choosing the right answer:

When an employee has a complaint about his assignment, the action which will *best* help him overcome his difficulty is to
- A. discuss his difficulty with his coworkers
- B. take the problem to the head of the organization
- C. take the problem to the person who gave him the assignment
- D. say nothing to anyone about his complaint

In answering this question, you should study each of the choices to find which is best. Consider choice "A" – Certainly an employee may discuss his complaint with fellow employees, but no change or improvement can result, and the complaint remains unresolved. Choice "B" is a poor choice since the head of the organization probably does not know what assignment you have been given, and taking your problem to him is known as "going over the head" of the supervisor. The supervisor, or person who made the assignment, is the person who can clarify it or correct any injustice. Choice "C" is, therefore, correct. To say nothing, as in choice "D," is unwise. Supervisors have and interest in knowing the problems employees are facing, and the employee is seeking a solution to his problem.

2) True/False Questions

The "true/false" or "right/wrong" form of question is sometimes used. Here a complete statement is given. Your job is to decide whether the statement is right or wrong.

SAMPLE: A roaming cell-phone call to a nearby city costs less than a non-roaming call to a distant city.

This statement is wrong, or false, since roaming calls are more expensive.

This is not a complete list of all possible question forms, although most of the others are variations of these common types. You will always get complete directions for answering questions. Be sure you understand *how* to mark your answers – ask questions until you do.

V. RECORDING YOUR ANSWERS

Computer terminals are used more and more today for many different kinds of exams.

For an examination with very few applicants, you may be told to record your answers in the test booklet itself. Separate answer sheets are much more common. If this separate answer sheet is to be scored by machine – and this is often the case – it is highly important that you mark your answers correctly in order to get credit.

An electronic scoring machine is often used in civil service offices because of the speed with which papers can be scored. Machine-scored answer sheets must be marked with a pencil, which will be given to you. This pencil has a high graphite content which responds to the electronic scoring machine. As a matter of fact, stray dots may register as answers, so do not let your pencil rest on the answer sheet while you are pondering the correct answer. Also, if your pencil lead breaks or is otherwise defective, ask for another.

Since the answer sheet will be dropped in a slot in the scoring machine, be careful not to bend the corners or get the paper crumpled.

The answer sheet normally has five vertical columns of numbers, with 30 numbers to a column. These numbers correspond to the question numbers in your test booklet. After each number, going across the page are four or five pairs of dotted lines. These short dotted lines have small letters or numbers above them. The first two pairs may also have a "T" or "F" above the letters. This indicates that the first two pairs only are to be used if the questions are of the true-false type. If the questions are multiple choice, disregard the "T" and "F" and pay attention only to the small letters or numbers.

Answer your questions in the manner of the sample that follows:

32. The largest city in the United States is
   A. Washington, D.C.
   B. New York City
   C. Chicago
   D. Detroit
   E. San Francisco

1) Choose the answer you think is best. (New York City is the largest, so "B" is correct.)
2) Find the row of dotted lines numbered the same as the question you are answering. (Find row number 32)
3) Find the pair of dotted lines corresponding to the answer. (Find the pair of lines under the mark "B.")
4) Make a solid black mark between the dotted lines.

VI. BEFORE THE TEST

Common sense will help you find procedures to follow to get ready for an examination. Too many of us, however, overlook these sensible measures. Indeed, nervousness and fatigue have been found to be the most serious reasons why applicants fail to do their best on civil service tests. Here is a list of reminders:

- Begin your preparation early – Don't wait until the last minute to go scurrying around for books and materials or to find out what the position is all about.
- Prepare continuously – An hour a night for a week is better than an all-night cram session. This has been definitely established. What is more, a night a week for a month will return better dividends than crowding your study into a shorter period of time.
- Locate the place of the exam – You have been sent a notice telling you when and where to report for the examination. If the location is in a different town or otherwise unfamiliar to you, it would be well to inquire the best route and learn something about the building.
- Relax the night before the test – Allow your mind to rest. Do not study at all that night. Plan some mild recreation or diversion; then go to bed early and get a good night's sleep.
- Get up early enough to make a leisurely trip to the place for the test – This way unforeseen events, traffic snarls, unfamiliar buildings, etc. will not upset you.
- Dress comfortably – A written test is not a fashion show. You will be known by number and not by name, so wear something comfortable.

- Leave excess paraphernalia at home – Shopping bags and odd bundles will get in your way. You need bring only the items mentioned in the official notice you received; usually everything you need is provided. Do not bring reference books to the exam. They will only confuse those last minutes and be taken away from you when in the test room.
- Arrive somewhat ahead of time – If because of transportation schedules you must get there very early, bring a newspaper or magazine to take your mind off yourself while waiting.
- Locate the examination room – When you have found the proper room, you will be directed to the seat or part of the room where you will sit. Sometimes you are given a sheet of instructions to read while you are waiting. Do not fill out any forms until you are told to do so; just read them and be prepared.
- Relax and prepare to listen to the instructions
- If you have any physical problem that may keep you from doing your best, be sure to tell the test administrator. If you are sick or in poor health, you really cannot do your best on the exam. You can come back and take the test some other time.

VII. AT THE TEST

The day of the test is here and you have the test booklet in your hand. The temptation to get going is very strong. Caution! There is more to success than knowing the right answers. You must know how to identify your papers and understand variations in the type of short-answer question used in this particular examination. Follow these suggestions for maximum results from your efforts:

1) Cooperate with the monitor

The test administrator has a duty to create a situation in which you can be as much at ease as possible. He will give instructions, tell you when to begin, check to see that you are marking your answer sheet correctly, and so on. He is not there to guard you, although he will see that your competitors do not take unfair advantage. He wants to help you do your best.

2) Listen to all instructions

Don't jump the gun! Wait until you understand all directions. In most civil service tests you get more time than you need to answer the questions. So don't be in a hurry. Read each word of instructions until you clearly understand the meaning. Study the examples, listen to all announcements and follow directions. Ask questions if you do not understand what to do.

3) Identify your papers

Civil service exams are usually identified by number only. You will be assigned a number; you must not put your name on your test papers. Be sure to copy your number correctly. Since more than one exam may be given, copy your exact examination title.

4) Plan your time

Unless you are told that a test is a "speed" or "rate of work" test, speed itself is usually not important. Time enough to answer all the questions will be provided, but this does not mean that you have all day. An overall time limit has been set. Divide the total time (in minutes) by the number of questions to determine the approximate time you have for each question.

5) Do not linger over difficult questions

If you come across a difficult question, mark it with a paper clip (useful to have along) and come back to it when you have been through the booklet. One caution if you do this – be sure to skip a number on your answer sheet as well. Check often to be sure that you have not lost your place and that you are marking in the row numbered the same as the question you are answering.

6) Read the questions

Be sure you know what the question asks! Many capable people are unsuccessful because they failed to *read* the questions correctly.

7) Answer all questions

Unless you have been instructed that a penalty will be deducted for incorrect answers, it is better to guess than to omit a question.

8) Speed tests

It is often better NOT to guess on speed tests. It has been found that on timed tests people are tempted to spend the last few seconds before time is called in marking answers at random – without even reading them – in the hope of picking up a few extra points. To discourage this practice, the instructions may warn you that your score will be "corrected" for guessing. That is, a penalty will be applied. The incorrect answers will be deducted from the correct ones, or some other penalty formula will be used.

9) Review your answers

If you finish before time is called, go back to the questions you guessed or omitted to give them further thought. Review other answers if you have time.

10) Return your test materials

If you are ready to leave before others have finished or time is called, take ALL your materials to the monitor and leave quietly. Never take any test material with you. The monitor can discover whose papers are not complete, and taking a test booklet may be grounds for disqualification.

VIII. EXAMINATION TECHNIQUES

1) Read the general instructions carefully. These are usually printed on the first page of the exam booklet. As a rule, these instructions refer to the timing of the examination; the fact that you should not start work until the signal and must stop work at a signal, etc. If there are any *special* instructions, such as a choice of questions to be answered, make sure that you note this instruction carefully.

2) When you are ready to start work on the examination, that is as soon as the signal has been given, read the instructions to each question booklet, underline any key words or phrases, such as *least, best, outline, describe* and the like. In this way you will tend to answer as requested rather than discover on reviewing your paper that you *listed without describing*, that you selected the *worst* choice rather than the *best* choice, etc.

3) If the examination is of the objective or multiple-choice type – that is, each question will also give a series of possible answers: A, B, C or D, and you are called upon to select the best answer and write the letter next to that answer on your answer paper – it is advisable to start answering each question in turn. There may be anywhere from 50 to 100 such questions in the three or four hours allotted and you can see how much time would be taken if you read through all the questions before beginning to answer any. Furthermore, if you come across a question or group of questions which you know would be difficult to answer, it would undoubtedly affect your handling of all the other questions.

4) If the examination is of the essay type and contains but a few questions, it is a moot point as to whether you should read all the questions before starting to answer any one. Of course, if you are given a choice – say five out of seven and the like – then it is essential to read all the questions so you can eliminate the two that are most difficult. If, however, you are asked to answer all the questions, there may be danger in trying to answer the easiest one first because you may find that you will spend too much time on it. The best technique is to answer the first question, then proceed to the second, etc.

5) Time your answers. Before the exam begins, write down the time it started, then add the time allowed for the examination and write down the time it must be completed, then divide the time available somewhat as follows:
   - If 3-1/2 hours are allowed, that would be 210 minutes. If you have 80 objective-type questions, that would be an average of 2-1/2 minutes per question. Allow yourself no more than 2 minutes per question, or a total of 160 minutes, which will permit about 50 minutes to review.
   - If for the time allotment of 210 minutes there are 7 essay questions to answer, that would average about 30 minutes a question. Give yourself only 25 minutes per question so that you have about 35 minutes to review.

6) The most important instruction is to *read each question* and make sure you know what is wanted. The second most important instruction is to *time yourself properly* so that you answer every question. The third most important instruction is to *answer every question*. Guess if you have to but include something for each question. Remember that you will receive no credit for a blank and will probably receive some credit if you write something in answer to an essay question. If you guess a letter – say "B" for a multiple-choice question – you may have guessed right. If you leave a blank as an answer to a multiple-choice question, the examiners may respect your feelings but it will not add a point to your score. Some exams may penalize you for wrong answers, so in such cases *only*, you may not want to guess unless you have some basis for your answer.

7) Suggestions
   a. Objective-type questions
      1. Examine the question booklet for proper sequence of pages and questions
      2. Read all instructions carefully
      3. Skip any question which seems too difficult; return to it after all other questions have been answered
      4. Apportion your time properly; do not spend too much time on any single question or group of questions

5. Note and underline key words – *all, most, fewest, least, best, worst, same, opposite*, etc.
6. Pay particular attention to negatives
7. Note unusual option, e.g., unduly long, short, complex, different or similar in content to the body of the question
8. Observe the use of "hedging" words – *probably, may, most likely*, etc.
9. Make sure that your answer is put next to the same number as the question
10. Do not second-guess unless you have good reason to believe the second answer is definitely more correct
11. Cross out original answer if you decide another answer is more accurate; do not erase until you are ready to hand your paper in
12. Answer all questions; guess unless instructed otherwise
13. Leave time for review

b. Essay questions
1. Read each question carefully
2. Determine exactly what is wanted. Underline key words or phrases.
3. Decide on outline or paragraph answer
4. Include many different points and elements unless asked to develop any one or two points or elements
5. Show impartiality by giving pros and cons unless directed to select one side only
6. Make and write down any assumptions you find necessary to answer the questions
7. Watch your English, grammar, punctuation and choice of words
8. Time your answers; don't crowd material

8) Answering the essay question

Most essay questions can be answered by framing the specific response around several key words or ideas. Here are a few such key words or ideas:

M's: manpower, materials, methods, money, management
P's: purpose, program, policy, plan, procedure, practice, problems, pitfalls, personnel, public relations

a. Six basic steps in handling problems:
1. Preliminary plan and background development
2. Collect information, data and facts
3. Analyze and interpret information, data and facts
4. Analyze and develop solutions as well as make recommendations
5. Prepare report and sell recommendations
6. Install recommendations and follow up effectiveness

b. Pitfalls to avoid
1. *Taking things for granted* – A statement of the situation does not necessarily imply that each of the elements is necessarily true; for example, a complaint may be invalid and biased so that all that can be taken for granted is that a complaint has been registered

2. *Considering only one side of a situation* – Wherever possible, indicate several alternatives and then point out the reasons you selected the best one
3. *Failing to indicate follow up* – Whenever your answer indicates action on your part, make certain that you will take proper follow-up action to see how successful your recommendations, procedures or actions turn out to be
4. *Taking too long in answering any single question* – Remember to time your answers properly

IX. AFTER THE TEST

Scoring procedures differ in detail among civil service jurisdictions although the general principles are the same. Whether the papers are hand-scored or graded by machine we have described, they are nearly always graded by number. That is, the person who marks the paper knows only the number – never the name – of the applicant. Not until all the papers have been graded will they be matched with names. If other tests, such as training and experience or oral interview ratings have been given, scores will be combined. Different parts of the examination usually have different weights. For example, the written test might count 60 percent of the final grade, and a rating of training and experience 40 percent. In many jurisdictions, veterans will have a certain number of points added to their grades.

After the final grade has been determined, the names are placed in grade order and an eligible list is established. There are various methods for resolving ties between those who get the same final grade – probably the most common is to place first the name of the person whose application was received first. Job offers are made from the eligible list in the order the names appear on it. You will be notified of your grade and your rank as soon as all these computations have been made. This will be done as rapidly as possible.

People who are found to meet the requirements in the announcement are called "eligibles." Their names are put on a list of eligible candidates. An eligible's chances of getting a job depend on how high he stands on this list and how fast agencies are filling jobs from the list.

When a job is to be filled from a list of eligibles, the agency asks for the names of people on the list of eligibles for that job. When the civil service commission receives this request, it sends to the agency the names of the three people highest on this list. Or, if the job to be filled has specialized requirements, the office sends the agency the names of the top three persons who meet these requirements from the general list.

The appointing officer makes a choice from among the three people whose names were sent to him. If the selected person accepts the appointment, the names of the others are put back on the list to be considered for future openings.

That is the rule in hiring from all kinds of eligible lists, whether they are for typist, carpenter, chemist, or something else. For every vacancy, the appointing officer has his choice of any one of the top three eligibles on the list. This explains why the person whose name is on top of the list sometimes does not get an appointment when some of the persons lower on the list do. If the appointing officer chooses the second or third eligible, the No. 1 eligible does not get a job at once, but stays on the list until he is appointed or the list is terminated.

X. HOW TO PASS THE INTERVIEW TEST

The examination for which you applied requires an oral interview test. You have already taken the written test and you are now being called for the interview test – the final part of the formal examination.

You may think that it is not possible to prepare for an interview test and that there are no procedures to follow during an interview. Our purpose is to point out some things you can do in advance that will help you and some good rules to follow and pitfalls to avoid while you are being interviewed.

What is an interview supposed to test?

The written examination is designed to test the technical knowledge and competence of the candidate; the oral is designed to evaluate intangible qualities, not readily measured otherwise, and to establish a list showing the relative fitness of each candidate – as measured against his competitors – for the position sought. Scoring is not on the basis of "right" and "wrong," but on a sliding scale of values ranging from "not passable" to "outstanding." As a matter of fact, it is possible to achieve a relatively low score without a single "incorrect" answer because of evident weakness in the qualities being measured.

Occasionally, an examination may consist entirely of an oral test – either an individual or a group oral. In such cases, information is sought concerning the technical knowledges and abilities of the candidate, since there has been no written examination for this purpose. More commonly, however, an oral test is used to supplement a written examination.

Who conducts interviews?

The composition of oral boards varies among different jurisdictions. In nearly all, a representative of the personnel department serves as chairman. One of the members of the board may be a representative of the department in which the candidate would work. In some cases, "outside experts" are used, and, frequently, a businessman or some other representative of the general public is asked to serve. Labor and management or other special groups may be represented. The aim is to secure the services of experts in the appropriate field.

However the board is composed, it is a good idea (and not at all improper or unethical) to ascertain in advance of the interview who the members are and what groups they represent. When you are introduced to them, you will have some idea of their backgrounds and interests, and at least you will not stutter and stammer over their names.

What should be done before the interview?

While knowledge about the board members is useful and takes some of the surprise element out of the interview, there is other preparation which is more substantive. It *is* possible to prepare for an oral interview – in several ways:

1) Keep a copy of your application and review it carefully before the interview

This may be the only document before the oral board, and the starting point of the interview. Know what education and experience you have listed there, and the sequence and dates of all of it. Sometimes the board will ask you to review the highlights of your experience for them; you should not have to hem and haw doing it.

2) Study the class specification and the examination announcement

Usually, the oral board has one or both of these to guide them. The qualities, characteristics or knowledges required by the position sought are stated in these documents. They offer valuable clues as to the nature of the oral interview. For example, if the job involves supervisory responsibilities, the announcement will usually indicate that knowledge of modern supervisory methods and the qualifications of the candidate as a supervisor will be tested. If so, you can expect such questions, frequently in the form of a hypothetical situation which you are expected to solve. NEVER go into an oral without knowledge of the duties and responsibilities of the job you seek.

3) Think through each qualification required

Try to visualize the kind of questions you would ask if you were a board member. How well could you answer them? Try especially to appraise your own knowledge and background in each area, *measured against the job sought*, and identify any areas in which you are weak. Be critical and realistic – do not flatter yourself.

4) Do some general reading in areas in which you feel you may be weak

For example, if the job involves supervision and your past experience has NOT, some general reading in supervisory methods and practices, particularly in the field of human relations, might be useful. Do NOT study agency procedures or detailed manuals. The oral board will be testing your understanding and capacity, not your memory.

5) Get a good night's sleep and watch your general health and mental attitude

You will want a clear head at the interview. Take care of a cold or any other minor ailment, and of course, no hangovers.

What should be done on the day of the interview?

Now comes the day of the interview itself. Give yourself plenty of time to get there. Plan to arrive somewhat ahead of the scheduled time, particularly if your appointment is in the fore part of the day. If a previous candidate fails to appear, the board might be ready for you a bit early. By early afternoon an oral board is almost invariably behind schedule if there are many candidates, and you may have to wait. Take along a book or magazine to read, or your application to review, but leave any extraneous material in the waiting room when you go in for your interview. In any event, relax and compose yourself.

The matter of dress is important. The board is forming impressions about you – from your experience, your manners, your attitude, and your appearance. Give your personal appearance careful attention. Dress your best, but not your flashiest. Choose conservative, appropriate clothing, and be sure it is immaculate. This is a business interview, and your appearance should indicate that you regard it as such. Besides, being well groomed and properly dressed will help boost your confidence.

Sooner or later, someone will call your name and escort you into the interview room. *This is it.* From here on you are on your own. It is too late for any more preparation. But remember, you asked for this opportunity to prove your fitness, and you are here because your request was granted.

What happens when you go in?

The usual sequence of events will be as follows: The clerk (who is often the board stenographer) will introduce you to the chairman of the oral board, who will introduce you to the other members of the board. Acknowledge the introductions before you sit down. Do not be surprised if you find a microphone facing you or a stenotypist sitting by. Oral interviews are usually recorded in the event of an appeal or other review.

Usually the chairman of the board will open the interview by reviewing the highlights of your education and work experience from your application – primarily for the benefit of the other members of the board, as well as to get the material into the record. Do not interrupt or comment unless there is an error or significant misinterpretation; if that is the case, do not hesitate. But do not quibble about insignificant matters. Also, he will usually ask you some question about your education, experience or your present job – partly to get you to start talking and to establish the interviewing "rapport." He may start the actual questioning, or turn it over to one of the other members. Frequently, each member undertakes the questioning on a particular area, one in which he is perhaps most competent, so you can expect each member to participate in the examination. Because time is limited, you may also expect some rather abrupt switches in the direction the questioning takes, so do not be upset by it. Normally, a board member will not pursue a single line of questioning unless he discovers a particular strength or weakness.

After each member has participated, the chairman will usually ask whether any member has any further questions, then will ask you if you have anything you wish to add. Unless you are expecting this question, it may floor you. Worse, it may start you off on an extended, extemporaneous speech. The board is not usually seeking more information. The question is principally to offer you a last opportunity to present further qualifications or to indicate that you have nothing to add. So, if you feel that a significant qualification or characteristic has been overlooked, it is proper to point it out in a sentence or so. Do not compliment the board on the thoroughness of their examination – they have been sketchy, and you know it. If you wish, merely say, "No thank you, I have nothing further to add." This is a point where you can "talk yourself out" of a good impression or fail to present an important bit of information. Remember, *you close the interview yourself*.

The chairman will then say, "That is all, Mr. _____, thank you." Do not be startled; the interview is over, and quicker than you think. Thank him, gather your belongings and take your leave. Save your sigh of relief for the other side of the door.

How to put your best foot forward

Throughout this entire process, you may feel that the board individually and collectively is trying to pierce your defenses, seek out your hidden weaknesses and embarrass and confuse you. Actually, this is not true. They are obliged to make an appraisal of your qualifications for the job you are seeking, and they want to see you in your best light. Remember, they must interview all candidates and a non-cooperative candidate may become a failure in spite of their best efforts to bring out his qualifications. Here are 15 suggestions that will help you:

1) Be natural – Keep your attitude confident, not cocky

If you are not confident that you can do the job, do not expect the board to be. Do not apologize for your weaknesses, try to bring out your strong points. The board is interested in a positive, not negative, presentation. Cockiness will antagonize any board member and make him wonder if you are covering up a weakness by a false show of strength.

2) Get comfortable, but don't lounge or sprawl

Sit erectly but not stiffly. A careless posture may lead the board to conclude that you are careless in other things, or at least that you are not impressed by the importance of the occasion. Either conclusion is natural, even if incorrect. Do not fuss with your clothing, a pencil or an ashtray. Your hands may occasionally be useful to emphasize a point; do not let them become a point of distraction.

3) Do not wisecrack or make small talk

This is a serious situation, and your attitude should show that you consider it as such. Further, the time of the board is limited – they do not want to waste it, and neither should you.

4) Do not exaggerate your experience or abilities

In the first place, from information in the application or other interviews and sources, the board may know more about you than you think. Secondly, you probably will not get away with it. An experienced board is rather adept at spotting such a situation, so do not take the chance.

5) If you know a board member, do not make a point of it, yet do not hide it

Certainly you are not fooling him, and probably not the other members of the board. Do not try to take advantage of your acquaintanceship – it will probably do you little good.

6) Do not dominate the interview

Let the board do that. They will give you the clues – do not assume that you have to do all the talking. Realize that the board has a number of questions to ask you, and do not try to take up all the interview time by showing off your extensive knowledge of the answer to the first one.

7) Be attentive

You only have 20 minutes or so, and you should keep your attention at its sharpest throughout. When a member is addressing a problem or question to you, give him your undivided attention. Address your reply principally to him, but do not exclude the other board members.

8) Do not interrupt

A board member may be stating a problem for you to analyze. He will ask you a question when the time comes. Let him state the problem, and wait for the question.

9) Make sure you understand the question

Do not try to answer until you are sure what the question is. If it is not clear, restate it in your own words or ask the board member to clarify it for you. However, do not haggle about minor elements.

10) Reply promptly but not hastily

A common entry on oral board rating sheets is "candidate responded readily," or "candidate hesitated in replies." Respond as promptly and quickly as you can, but do not jump to a hasty, ill-considered answer.

11) Do not be peremptory in your answers

A brief answer is proper – but do not fire your answer back. That is a losing game from your point of view. The board member can probably ask questions much faster than you can answer them.

12) Do not try to create the answer you think the board member wants

He is interested in what kind of mind you have and how it works – not in playing games. Furthermore, he can usually spot this practice and will actually grade you down on it.

13) Do not switch sides in your reply merely to agree with a board member

Frequently, a member will take a contrary position merely to draw you out and to see if you are willing and able to defend your point of view. Do not start a debate, yet do not surrender a good position. If a position is worth taking, it is worth defending.

14) Do not be afraid to admit an error in judgment if you are shown to be wrong

The board knows that you are forced to reply without any opportunity for careful consideration. Your answer may be demonstrably wrong. If so, admit it and get on with the interview.

15) Do not dwell at length on your present job

The opening question may relate to your present assignment. Answer the question but do not go into an extended discussion. You are being examined for a *new* job, not your present one. As a matter of fact, try to phrase ALL your answers in terms of the job for which you are being examined.

Basis of Rating

Probably you will forget most of these "do's" and "don'ts" when you walk into the oral interview room. Even remembering them all will not ensure you a passing grade. Perhaps you did not have the qualifications in the first place. But remembering them will help you to put your best foot forward, without treading on the toes of the board members.

Rumor and popular opinion to the contrary notwithstanding, an oral board wants you to make the best appearance possible. They know you are under pressure – but they also want to see how you respond to it as a guide to what your reaction would be under the pressures of the job you seek. They will be influenced by the degree of poise you display, the personal traits you show and the manner in which you respond.

ABOUT THIS BOOK

This book contains tests divided into Examination Sections. Go through each test, answering every question in the margin. We have also attached a sample answer sheet at the back of the book that can be removed and used. At the end of each test look at the answer key and check your answers. On the ones you got wrong, look at the right answer choice and learn. Do not fill in the answers first. Do not memorize the questions and answers, but understand the answer and principles involved. On your test, the questions will likely be different from the samples. Questions are changed and new ones added. If you understand these past questions you should have success with any changes that arise. Tests may consist of several types of questions. We have additional books on each subject should more study be advisable or necessary for you. Finally, the more you study, the better prepared you will be. This book is intended to be the last thing you study before you walk into the examination room. Prior study of relevant texts is also recommended. NLC publishes some of these in our Fundamental Series. Knowledge and good sense are important factors in passing your exam. Good luck also helps. So now study this Passbook, absorb the material contained within and take that knowledge into the examination. Then do your best to pass that exam.

EXAMINATION SECTION

EXAMINATION SECTION
TEST 1

DIRECTIONS: Each question or incomplete statement is followed by several suggested answers or completions. Select the one that BEST answers the question or completes the statement. *PRINT THE LETTER OF THE CORRECT ANSWER IN THE SPACE AT THE RIGHT.*

1. In a hand tap set, the tap used to start a thread in a drilled hole is known as a _____ tap.

    A. taper B. plug C. small D. bottoming

2. The type of fastener used to fasten thin gauge metal to wood backing, without drilling, is known as a

    A. sheet metal screw B. cap screw
    C. wood screw D. screw nail

3. Set screws are usually used for

    A. fastening collars to shafts
    B. holding thin metal sheets together
    C. holding roller bearings to shafts
    D. clamping together steel angles

4. When using a pedestal type grinding wheel, the operator should always

    A. have the work-rest loose
    B. avoid striking the rotating wheel
    C. increase the speed above normal
    D. use a respirator

5. A flat cold chisel is the type of chisel usually used for chipping and/or cutting

    A. filleted corners B. flat surfaces
    C. V-shaped grooves D. narrow grooves

6. The type of chisel that is usually used to cut keyways in cast iron is generally known as a _____ chisel.

    A. star B. cold
    C. cape D. diamond point

7. The primary difference between brazing and soldering is that brazing requires

    A. greater heat
    B. a smaller soldering iron
    C. the use of soft solder
    D. the use of 50-50 solder

Questions 8-9.

DIRECTIONS: Questions 8 and 9 refer to the sketch below.

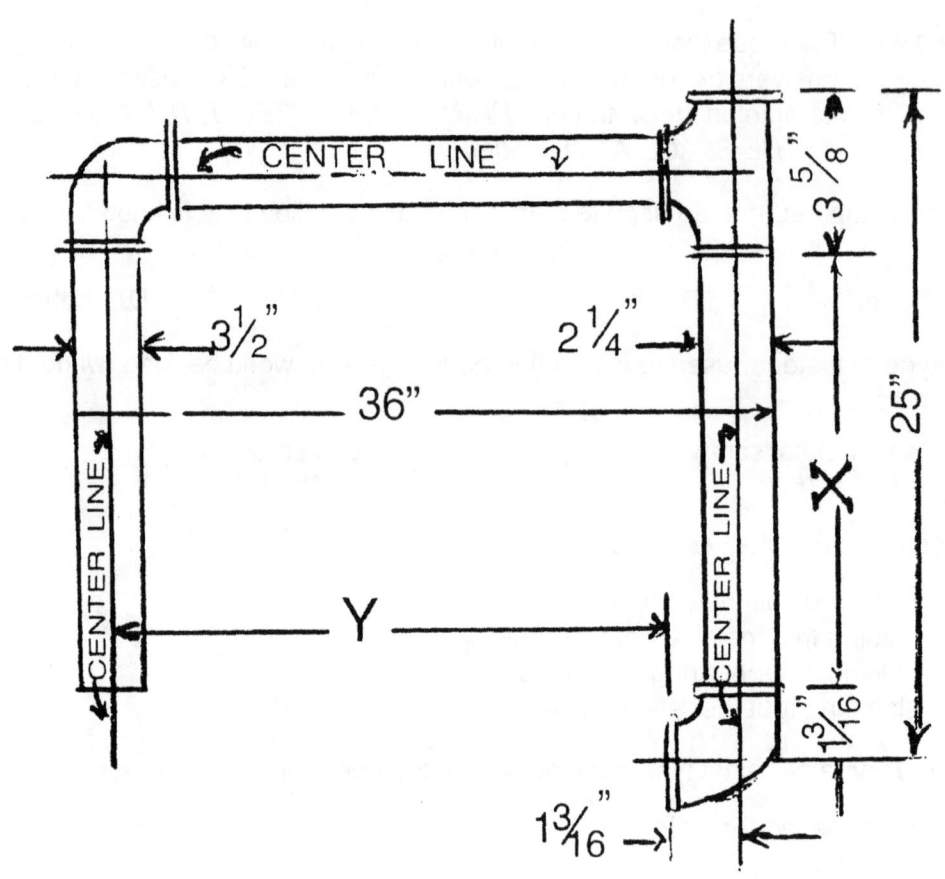

8. In the above sketch, the dimension X, in inches, is

   A. 19 13/16   B. 20 3/16   C. 20 3/8   D. 21 3/16

9. In the above sketch, the dimension Y, in inches, is

   A. 30 7/16   B. 31 5/16   C. 31 7/16   D. 31 15/16

10. A piece of 4" cast iron pipe may BEST be cut with a

    A. hacksaw having a blade with 32 teeth per inch
    B. hacksaw having a blade with 14 teeth per inch
    C. hammer and round nose chisel
    D. hammer and diamond point chisel

11. A four-inch length of straight pipe, threaded on both ends, is generally called a

    A. sleeve   B. nipple   C. stud   D. extension

12. A pipe fitting that is usually used to join together two threaded pipes of the same diameter is known as a

    A. union
    B. straight T with reducer leg
    C. nipple
    D. straight tee

13. A pipe fitting that is generally used to join two threaded pipes of different diameters is called a(n)   13.____

    A. close nipple   B. union
    C. adapter   D. reducer

14. A 90° pipe fitting that has a male thread at one end and a female thread at the other end is generally known as a 90°   14.____

    A. elbow   B. street elbow
    C. reducing ell   D. long radius ell

15. Paints generally used for covering outside pipes or sheet iron are composed of   15.____

    A. mineral pigments, organic vehicles and thinners
    B. resins dissolved in organic thinners
    C. pigmented oil and linseed oil
    D. lac gum dissolved in alcohol

16. A painted panel of wood after being exposed to the atmosphere becomes leather-like in appearance.   16.____
    This paint failure is called

    A. checking   B. alligatoring
    C. wrinkling   D. chalking

17. Paint brushes that are used for alkyd paints are usually cleaned with   17.____

    A. soap and water
    B. turpentine and mineral spirits
    C. linseed oil
    D. denatured alcohol mixed with water

18. Of the following statements, the one which is INCORRECT concerning painting practices is: 18.____

    A. Zinc dust primers are used for galvanized iron and sheet zinc
    B. Red lead paint is usually used as a final coat for steel surfaces
    C. Rubber-base paints may be applied to dry or damp walls
    D. Freshly varnished work should be kept clean and in a dust-free space

19. A white paint, that can cover 500 square feet of surface per gallon, is used to paint the crosswalks at street intersections.   19.____
    If the area at each intersection is equal to 300 square feet, the number of gallons required to paint 50 intersections is MOST NEARLY

    A. 10   B. 20   C. 30   D. 40

20. Of the following methods of splicing insulated electrical wires, the one which is recommended is to strip the ends, twist them together,   20.____

    A. and cover with friction tape
    B. solder and cover with friction tape
    C. shellac and cover with rubber tape
    D. solder, cover with rubber tape, and then with friction tape

21. If two 120V incandescent lamps are connected in parallel in a 120V circuit, the result will MOST likely be that the

    A. lamps will light up to normal brilliancy
    B. voltage across each lamp will be reduced to 60 volts
    C. life of each lamp will be doubled
    D. lamp will light up to 1/2 their normal brilliancy

22. Portable electric hand tools are usually polarized by means of a(n)

    A. circuit breaker   B. fuse
    C. three-prong plug   D. overload switch

23. The flux generally used when soldering electrical copper connections is

    A. zinc chloride
    B. an alcoholic solution of resin
    C. muriatic acid
    D. stearin

24. Fuses in the electric wiring systems of a car or truck are MAINLY used for the purpose of

    A. making it easy to disconnect some of the lights while allowing others to burn
    B. reducing the amount of current used, in order to save the battery
    C. automatically opening the circuit in case of an overload
    D. preventing the battery from overcharging under high speed

25. The BEST way to fasten electric conduit to an outlet box is by means of a

    A. bushing on the end of the conduit
    B. locknut on the outside of the box
    C. bushing on the inside and a locknut on the outside
    D. locknut on the inside and a bushing on the outside

26. The GREATEST hazard of explosion exists whenever

    A. gasoline is stored in airtight tanks
    B. a pool of gasoline is exposed to air
    C. gasoline is in a partially-full closed tank
    D. gasoline comes into contact with oil

27.

    ① (slotted)   ② (phillips)   ③ (hex)   ④ (two holes)

    In the above sketch, the head of a screw which represents an alien-head screw is numbered

    A. 1   B. 2   C. 3   D. 4

28. A ratchet wrench is usually used when

   A. the surface finish of a bolt must be preserved
   B. only a short swing of the wrench handle is permissible
   C. nuts are practically inaccessible
   D. tightening compression fittings

29. Grout in construction work is usually used to

   A. increase the strength of concrete
   B. seal porous timber surfaces
   C. prime concrete sidewalks
   D. fill spaces between brick or stone joints

30. A cutting tool that is being ground on an emery wheel is usually cooled by immersing it in

   A. oil
   B. water
   C. kerosene
   D. turpentine

31. Of the following statements concerning the use of screwdrivers, the one which is INCORRECT is:

   A. Always use a screwdriver with a blade that fits the screw to be turned
   B. Hold the work in one hand while turning the screwdriver with the other
   C. A screwdriver with an insulated handle should be used for making electrical repairs
   D. A screwdriver should not be used as a chisel or hammer

32. A miter box is usually used for

   A. making diagonal cuts
   B. holding the flux in soldering
   C. storing small machine screws
   D. storing precision tools

Questions 33-38.

DIRECTIONS: Questions 33 through 38, inclusive, should be answered in accordance with the following paragraph.

   It is important that traffic signals be regularly and effectively maintained. Signals with impaired efficiency cannot be expected to command desired respect. Poorly maintained traffic signs create disrespect in the minds of those who are to obey them and thereby reduce the effectiveness and authority of the signs. Maintenance should receive paramount consideration in the design and purchase of traffic signal equipment. The initial step in a good maintenance program for traffic signals is the establishment of a maintenance record. This record should show the cost of operation and maintenance of different types of equipment. It should give complete information regarding signal operations and indicate where defective planning exists in maintenance programs.

33. The word *effectively,* as used in the above paragraph means MOST NEARLY

   A. occasionally
   B. properly
   C. expensively
   D. cheaply

34. The word *impaired,* as used in the above paragraph, means MOST NEARLY   34.____

    A. reduced   B. increased   C. constant   D. high

35. The word *desired,* as used in the above paragraph, means MOST NEARLY   35.____

    A. public   B. complete   C. wanted   D. enough

36. The word *paramount,* as used in the above paragraph, means MOST NEARLY   36.____

    A. little   B. chief   C. excessive   D. some

37. The word *initial,* as used in the above paragraph, means MOST NEARLY   37.____

    A. first   B. final
    C. determining   D. most important

38. The word *defective,* as used in the above paragraph, means MOST NEARLY   38.____

    A. suitable   B. real   C. good   D. faulty

39. A half round file is usually used for   39.____

    A. removing stock rapidly
    B. clearing out square corners
    C. finishing the bottoms of narrow slots
    D. finishing concave surfaces

40. For finishing flat metal surfaces, the type of file usually used is the _____ file.   40.____

    A. pillar   B. hand   C. square   D. drill

KEY (CORRECT ANSWERS)

1. A	11. B	21. A	31. B
2. D	12. A	22. C	32. A
3. A	13. D	23. B	33. B
4. B	14. B	24. C	34. A
5. B	15. A	25. C	35. C
6. C	16. C	26. B	36. B
7. A	17. B	27. C	37. A
8. B	18. B	28. B	38. D
9. D	19. C	29. D	39. D
10. D	20. D	30. B	40. B

TEST 2

DIRECTIONS: Each question or incomplete statement is followed by several suggested answers or completions. Select the one that BEST answers the question or completes the statement. *PRINT THE LETTER OF THE CORRECT ANSWER IN THE SPACE AT THE RIGHT.*

1. The type of pliers usually used for holding or bending thin flat iron stock is known as 1.____
   - A. diagonal pliers
   - B. round nose pliers
   - C. nippers
   - D. side cutting pliers

2. An auger bit is usually used for boring a hole in 2.____
   - A. brass
   - B. concrete
   - C. wood
   - D. steel

3. The dimension 45" expressed in feet is MOST NEARLY 3.____
   - A. 3 1/3
   - B. 3 1/2
   - C. 3 3/4
   - D. 3 7/8

4. The type of hand saw that is used to cut wood along the grain is generally known as a _____ saw. 4.____
   - A. band
   - B. rip
   - C. back
   - D. cross cut

5. The LEAST likely cause for the breaking of hacksaw blades is 5.____
   - A. using a fine-toothed blade on thin work
   - B. using a coarse-toothed blade on thin work
   - C. working with a blade that is tightly drawn in the hacksaw frame
   - D. applying too much pressure on the work

6. A 1:3:5 mixture of concrete generally refers to a mixture of 1 part of _____, 3 parts of _____, 5 parts of _____. 6.____
   - A. gravel, sand, cement
   - B. sand, cement, gravel
   - C. water, cement, gravel
   - D. cement, sand, gravel

7. 85 percent of $5,250 is MOST NEARLY 7.____
   - A. $3,463.50
   - B. $4,361.50
   - C. $4,462.50
   - D. $4,666.50

8. A scriber is usually used for 8.____
   - A. starting a hole in iron
   - B. measuring lengths
   - C. cleaning threads
   - D. layout work

9. The gauge of an iron sheet indicates its 9.____
   - A. thickness
   - B. length
   - C. weight per square inch
   - D. width

10. The type of gears used on the ends of two intersecting shafts 90° to each other for transmitting motion are known as 10.____
    - A. spur
    - B. bevel
    - C. spline
    - D. spiral

11. If the shortest distance between the edges of two holes drilled in a flat steel plate is 1 1/2" and the diameters of the holes are 3/4" and 1", the distance between centers is MOST NEARLY

    A. 2 1/8"   B. 2 1/4"   C. 2 3/8"   D. 2 3/4"

12. A flat head screw that is identified as a 1/4X 20 - 1" long screw is MOST likely a _____ screw.

    A. wood
    B. sheet metal
    C. cap
    D. machine

13. If your foreman informs you that a traffic signal was obliterated, he MOST likely means that the traffic signal was

    A. stolen   B. obsolete   C. loose   D. destroyed

14. Of the following statements, the one which is MOST correct concerning a *regulatory* traffic sign is that the sign

    A. if disregarded by the driver, is punishable as a misdemeanor
    B. calls attention to conditions that are potentially hazardous to traffic
    C. shows route designations and directions
    D. shows points of interest and other geographical information

15. The MAIN reason for the alternate-side-of-the-street parking regulations is to

    A. facilitate the cleaning of streets
    B. allow room for moving traffic
    C. allow room for delivery trucks
    D. provide space for children to play

16. The geometrical shape of *STOP* signs if

    A. octagonal
    B. triangular
    C. diamond
    D. rectangular

17. In an engine, the MAIN purpose for using oil as a lubricant is to keep

    A. the engine parts from rusting
    B. a film between the moving parts
    C. the internal parts clean, by flushing them
    D. the vibration down

18. The QUICKEST method of determining a defective spark plug is to

    A. take out the spark plugs and examine them
    B. drive to the garage and let a mechanic tell you
    C. short circuit the spark plugs one at a time with an insulated screwdriver
    D. replace all the spark plugs with new ones

19. The device that controls the charging rate of a generator in the generator-battery circuit of an automotive engine is usually the

    A. ignition coil
    B. generator regulator
    C. condenser
    D. generator solenoid

20. The device used with a gasoline engine to change the liquid fuel into vapor and mix it with air is called a(n) 20._____

    A. fuel pump   B. automatic choke
    C. carburetor   D. vapor regulator

21. The gap between the electrodes of a spark plug is usually measured with a 21._____

    A. feeler gauge   B. flat stock
    C. depth gauge   D. caliper

22. The proper spark plug gap for MOST truck engines is approximately 22._____

    A. .015"   B. .018"   C. .030"   D. .042"

23. A truck mounted air compressor that supplies air to a number of pneumatic tools is usually set to deliver air at APPROXIMATELY _____ psi. 23._____

    A. 30   B. 50   C. 90   D. 160

Questions 24-25.

DIRECTIONS: Questions 24 and 25 refer to the sketch below depicting a street intersection.

24. In the above sketch, the southeast corner is numbered 24._____

    A. 1   B. 2   C. 3   D. 4

25. In the above sketch, the northwest corner is numbered 25._____

    A. 1   B. 2   C. 3   D. 4

26. The proper position to place yourself when lifting a heavy box from the floor is to 26._____

    A. squat down, bend knees, keep back straight and lift
    B. bend down, hunch back, and lift

C. keep feet away from object, bend back, and lift
D. bend, and use the back muscles when lifting

Questions 27-28.

DIRECTIONS: Questions 27 and 28 refer to the sketches immediately below.

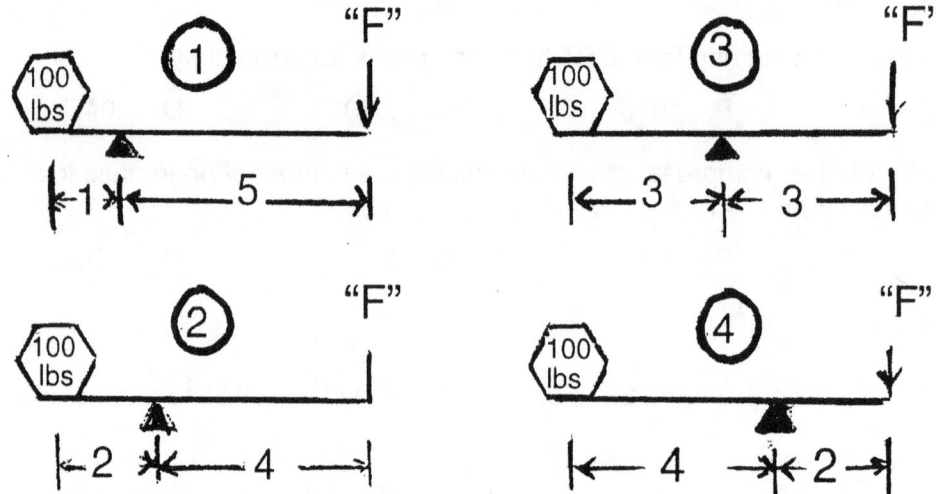

27. The one of the above sketches in which the LEAST force F that is necessary to raise the 100 lb. weight is shown in sketch number   27.____

    A. 1   B. 2   C. 3   D. 4

28. The one of the above sketches in which the MOST force F that is necessary to raise the 100 lb. weight is shown in sketch number   28.____

    A. 1   B. 2   C. 3   D. 4

29. In the sketch shown at the right, the SMALLEST or LEAST pull P in pounds required to hoist a load of 1 1/2 tons is MOST NEARLY   29.____

    A. 500
    B. 1,000
    C. 1,500
    D. 2,000

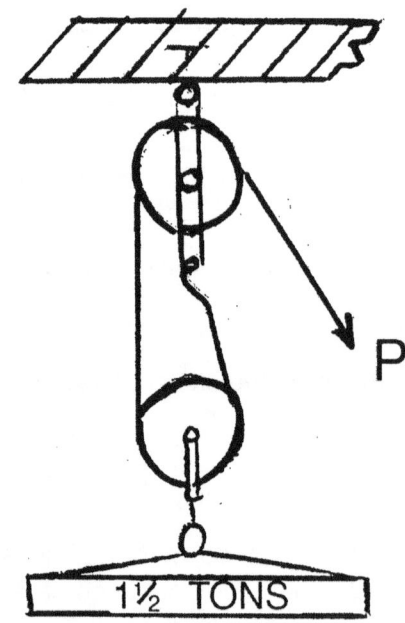

30. Of the following statements, the one which is INCORRECT is: Fibre rope

    A. should be stored in an air-tight container
    B. should never be stored on the ground
    C. is approximately 10% stronger when wet
    D. should be inspected periodically

31. The term *mousing,* as used in rigging, means MOST NEARLY

    A. temporarily attaching a rope to a hook
    B. attaching a rope to a tackle block
    C. securing a grip on a rope under strain
    D. placing rope yarn on a hook to prevent load from becoming detached

32. The safe distance that the bottom of a ladder, the top of which is placed against a wall or pole must extend out from the base of the wall or pole, is usually _____ the length of the ladder.

    A. 1/2 B. 1/4 C. 1/6 D. 1/8

33. Of the following painting materials, the one which should NOT be used to treat or cover wood ladders is

    A. linseed oil   B. oil paint
    C. shellac   D. varnish

34. A knot that has a non-slipping eye, will not jam, and is easily untied is generally known as a(n)

    A. sheet bend   B. granny
    C. bowline   D. overhand knot

35. A sheepshank knot is PRINCIPALLY used for

    A. shortening a rope without cutting it
    B. fastening a rope at right angles to a post
    C. attaching a rope to a ring
    D. joining large hawsers

36. Of the following procedures for softening a piece of steel, good practice is to FIRST heat the steel and then

    A. cool it rapidly
    B. dip it in cold water
    C. cool it slowly
    D. cool it in a cold solution of salt

37. Of the following types of measuring rules, the one which can BEST be used to measure directly the circumference of a 4-inch diameter pipe is the _____ rule.

    A. zig-zag   B. folding
    C. caliper   D. push-pull

38. The painting of traffic safety lines and pedestrian crosswalks at busy intersections is one of the jobs of a traffic device maintainer.
    The work crew usually protects itself from traffic by

    A. re-routing the traffic at the next intersection
    B. lengthening the time for the *Stop* signal on the traffic light
    C. wearing bright yellow work clothes
    D. placing safety cones to divert traffic away from the work area

38.____

39. An unloader is a device that is usually found on a(n)

    A. pneumatic tool   B. air compressor
    C. storage tank   D. block and fall

39.____

40. A device that can be used repeatedly for marking out shapes on materials is generally called a

    A. blueprint   B. tracing   C. scantling   D. template

40.____

KEY (CORRECT ANSWERS)

1.	D	11.	C	21.	A	31.	D
2.	C	12.	D	22.	C	32.	B
3.	C	13.	D	23.	C	33.	B
4.	B	14.	A	24.	D	34.	C
5.	A	15.	A	25.	A	35.	A
6.	D	16.	A	26.	A	36.	C
7.	C	17.	B	27.	A	37.	D
8.	D	18.	C	28.	D	38.	D
9.	A	19.	B	29.	C	39.	B
10.	B	20.	C	30.	A	40.	D

EXAMINATION SECTION
TEST 1

DIRECTIONS: Each question or incomplete statement is followed by several suggested answers or completions. Select the one that BEST answers the question or completes the statement. *PRINT THE LETTER OF THE CORRECT ANSWER IN THE SPACE AT THE RIGHT.*

1. When making a preliminary inspection of a new street marking job, the FIRST thing to check is whether

    A. the location is correct
    B. all dimensions are correct
    C. the right paint is specified
    D. traffic can easily be controlled

    1.____

2. After a preliminary inspection of a new street marking job has been made and it has been found that it can be laid out exactly as shown in the drawings received from Plans and Surveys, the site should be reinspected on the first day of actual work to check that

    A. the dimensions are correct according to the plans
    B. the orientation has not changed
    C. excavation work that did not exist on his first inspection does not obstruct his work
    D. the traffic can easily be controlled

    2.____

3. Of the following, it is MOST important when inspecting the installation of a sign in a garage or on a street to check for the _____ the sign.

    A. correct width of
    B. correct area of
    C. correct mounting height of
    D. removal of all scuff marks below

    3.____

4. When inspecting a job site in an off-street parking garage prior to starting a new job involving markings, the FIRST thing to look for is

    A. obstructions such as beams which will require that the layout be altered
    B. oil on the floor
    C. paint splashes on the floor
    D. vehicles which must be moved

    4.____

5. The one of the following items which should be checked on a job involving the installation of custom-made highway guide signs but which need NOT be checked during the installation of street regulatory signs is the _____ of the sign.

    A. color   B. wording and spelling
    C. width   D. area

    5.____

6. Assume that you are facing east while standing on the northwest corner of the intersection of two streets. One of these streets runs north and south, and the other runs east and west.
The SOUTHWEST corner of this intersection is

    6.____

13

A. *directly* across the street in front of you
B. *directly* across the street to your right
C. *diagonally* across the intersection from you
D. *directly* across the street to your left

7. A street running north and south intersects a street running east and west. Four men designated as A, B, C, and D are each on a different corner of the intersection. A is on the NW corner and faces east; B is on the SW corner and faces north; C is on the SE corner and faces west; and D is on the NE corner and faces west.
The two men who are facing DIRECTLY toward each other are

A. A and B   B. B and C   C. C and D   D. A and D

8. Of the following, the MOST important item to check during a routine inspection of an air compressor is the

A. amount of air used daily
B. number of hours it has been operated
C. diaphragm diameter
D. condition of the paint finish

9. Assume that a crew assigned to you goes out to paint some street markings on a street which has a great deal of traffic.
The traffic should be diverted away from the working area by means of

A. Class I barricades
B. Class II barricades
C. Class I barricades and cones
D. cones

10. Assume that an extensive area within an off-street parking facility has caved in. Until repairs are completed, cars should be kept away from this area by means of

A. Class I barricades
B. Class I barricades and flasher lights
C. Class II barricades and cones
D. warning signs and Class I barricades

11. A line of traffic cones, being used to divert traffic fron men painting cross-walks in the lane nearest the curb, should begin at the curb at a point whose distance fron the working area is _____ feet, and the cones should be _____ feet apart.

A. 40; 10   B. 60; 15   C. 80; 15   D. 100; 10

12. Crews doing street marking work at night should wear

A. gray coveralls and set out traffic cones to divert traffic away from the area
B. reflectorized vests and set out traffic cones to divert traffic away from the area
C. bright yellow helmets and gray coveralls
D. bright blue helmets and set out traffic cones to divert traffic away from the area

13. Assume that the top of a 12 foot ladder is to be placed against a wall.
    The RECOMMENDED safe practice is that the ladder should be placed so that the distance from the bottom of the ladder to the base of the wall is _____ ft.

    A. 1   B. 2   C. 3   D. 5

14. According to the State Vehicle and Traffic Law, when driving at a speed of 40 miles per hour along a dry road, the driver should maintain a distance between his car and the car immediately ahead of him of AT LEAST _____ car lengths.

    A. 2   B. 3   C. 4   D. 5

15. Assume that a man has been knocked unconscious.
    Which of the following should NOT be done to the victim?

    A. Give him something to drink
    B. Hold a handkerchief with spirits of ammonia under his nose if he is breathing
    C. Keep him covered with a blanket
    D. Give him artificial respiration if he is not breathing

16. A paint sprayer may have gauges showing the pressure of the tank, the paint pressure, and the atomizer pressure. When the sprayer is operating properly, the

    A. paint pressure is higher than the tank pressure
    B. atomizer pressure is higher than the tank pressure
    C. paint and atomizer pressures are equal
    D. atomizer pressure is higher than the paint pressure

17. A certain paint can cover 310 square feet per gallon. The number of gallons of this paint required to paint 200 lines each 6 inches wide and 18 feet-6 inches long is MOST NEARLY

    A. 2   B. 4   C. 6   D. 8

18. Paint brushes that are used with an oil-based paint are USUALLY cleaned with

    A. turpentine   B. linseed oil
    C. acetone   D. alcohol

19. The air in an air compressor cylinder is DIRECTLY compressed by the

    A. pressure switch B. surge chamber
    C. cam   D. piston

20. The part which permits the motor of an air compressor to start free of load regardless of the tank pressure is the

    A. unloader valve   B. surge tank
    C. pressure switch D. drain cock

21. Assume that instead of spraying paint properly, a paint sprayer ejects a solid stream of paint from its nozzle. The one of the following that may cause this condition is

    A. compressor tank pressure is too high
    B. compressor tank pressure is lower than the atomizer pressure
    C. atomizer pressure is higher than the paint pressure
    D. atomizer pressure is too low

22. The one of the following which is a *regulatory* sign is the

    A. bump sign   B. low clearance sign
    C. route marker   D. stop sign

22.____

23. The one of the following which is a *regulatory* sign is the _____ sign.

    A. yield   B. stop ahead
    C. side road   D. slippery when wet

23.____

24. The one of the following signs which is octagonal is the _____ sign.

    A. speed limit   B. stop ahead
    C. road narrows   D. stop

24.____

25. Of the following statements, the one which gives the function of a *warning* sign is that this sign

    A. indicates route designations, destinations, or distances
    B. gives the driver notice of laws or regulations that apply at a given place, disregard of which is punishable as a violation or a misdemeanor
    C. calls attention to conditions in or adjacent to a street that are potentially hazardous to traffic
    D. indicates points of interest or geographical locations

25.____

26. The regulation manual on temporary traffic control of the department of traffic defines Class II barricades as being of the *horse* type with only one rail.
It further specifies that the rail should be marked on

    A. *one* side with 3" vertical red and white, black and white, or black and yellow reflectorized stripes
    B. *both* sides with 3" vertical red and white, black and white, or black and yellow stripes
    C. *both* sides with 6" reflectorized red and white, black and white, or black and yellow stripes sloping at an angle of 45
    D. *both* sides with 6" vertical red and white or black and white stripes

26.____

27. Silk screening is a method of

    A. temporarily concealing signs already erected but not ready to be used
    B. painting signs
    C. protecting newly painted crosswalks until they dry
    D. protecting reflectorized signs from dust

27.____

28. The blade of a snow plow is USUALLY made of

    A. monel   B. steel
    C. tungsten carbide   D. beryllium

28.____

29. To PROPERLY check the lifting device of a snow plow at the beginning of the snow season, the plow blade should be

    A. raised and kept in that position for at least three minutes in order to detect leaks in the system
    B. raised by the lifting device once to see if it operates

29.____

C. dropped quickly after being brought to the raised position
D. raised and lowered and then the operation should be repeated

30. At the present time, the department of traffic USUALLY reflectorizes signs by   30._____

    A. coating the portion of the sign to be reflectorized with very tiny glass beads held by an adhesive base
    B. outlining the reflectorized portion of the sign with large glass *bull's eyes*
    C. making the reflectorized portion of the sign with *Scotch Lite*
    D. painting the reflectorized portion of the sign with *Luminar*

KEY (CORRECT ANSWERS)

1. A	11. D	21. D
2. C	12. B	22. D
3. C	13. C	23. A
4. A	14. C	24. D
5. B	15. A	25. C
6. B	16. D	26. C
7. D	17. C	27. B
8. B	18. A	28. B
9. D	19. D	29. A
10. C	20. A	30. C

TEST 2

DIRECTIONS: Each question or incomplete statement is followed by several suggested answers or completions. Select the one that BEST answers the question or completes the statement. *PRINT THE LETTER OF THE CORRECT ANSWER IN THE SPACE AT THE RIGHT.*

1. The material which causes the hydraulic plunger of a heavy duty hydraulic jack to move is
   A. oil
   b. petrolatum
   C. alcohol
   D. glycerol

   1.____

2. "Vapor Lock" will DIRECTLY affect the operation of
   A. air compressors
   B. pneumatic hammers
   C. paint sprayers
   D. automobiles

   2.____

3. Of the following grades of SAE crankcase oils, the one which is RECOMMENDED for year-round use is
   A. 10W-30
   B. 30
   C. 20W
   D. 10W

   3.____

4. Of the following, wheel misalignment in an automobile USUALLY results in
   A. frequent stalling
   B. improper clutch action
   C. rapid tire wear
   D. impaired shock absorber action

   4.____

5. Of the following, the EASIEST method of locating a defective spark plug in a gasoline engine is to
   A. take out all the spark plugs and examine them
   B. short circuit the spark plugs one at a time
   C. replace all of the spark plugs with new ones
   D. rotate all the spark plugs

   5.____

6. The one of the following conditions which may cause the fuel mixture in a gasoline engine to be too rich is
   A. water in the gasoline
   B. a dirty air cleaner
   C. a punctured muffler
   D. vapor lock in the fuel line

   6.____

7. If the battery of a car is constantly running dry, the one of the following items which should be checked FIRST is the
   A. generator
   B. ignition switch
   C. relay
   D. voltage regulator

   7.____

8. In a gasoline engine, the throttle vale is a part of the
   A. fuel tank
   B. carbureto
   C. crankcase
   D. water radiator

   8.____

9. If a car does not start on damp days, the trouble is MOST likely in the _____ system. 9.____
   A. ignition   B. fuel   C. lubricating   D. cooling

10. The one of the following terms that applies to the relationship between the front axle and the steering mechanism of an automobile is 10.____
    A. camber   B. armature   C. crankshaft   D. camshaft

11. The function of a carburetor on a gasoline engine is to 11.____
    A. filter the gasoline
    B. mix air and gasoline in the correct proportions
    C. pump the gasoline into the cylinder
    D. filter the air coming into the engine

12. An automotive ignition coil is used in the electrical system of a gasoline engine to 12.____
    A. reduce arcing across the breaker points
    B. transformers low voltage to high voltage
    C. operate the ignition switch
    D. charge the battery

13. The purpose of the thermostat in the cooling system of a gasoline engine is to 13.____
    A. indicate the temperature of the cooling water
    B. control water flow so as to prevent excessive pressure in the radiator
    C. prevent overheating of the cooling water
    D. prevent circulation of the cooling water when the engine is cold

14. Of the following sets of items, the BEST one to use to clean and adjust ignition points is 14.____
    A. crescent wrench, V-block, and sandpaper
    B. screwdriver, feeler gauge, and point file
    C. scraper, micrometer, and sandpaper
    D. pincers, micrometer, and emery cloth

15. The MAIN reason for not allowing oily rags to accumulate in storage closets is that 15.____
    A. a rancid odor will develop near the closet
    B. the closet will look messy
    C. oil will drip onto the floor
    D. a fire may start by spontaneous combustion

16. A certain paint can cover 310 square feet per gallon. The number of gallons of this paint required to paint 200 lines each 6 inches wide and 18 feet, 6 inches long is MOST nearly 16.____
    A. 2   B. 4   C. 6   D. 8

17. Paint brushes that are used with an oil-based paint are usually cleaned with 17.____
    A. turpentine   B. linseed oil   C. acetone   D. alcohol

18. Assume that, while you are using an electric drill with a long electric cord, the drill suddenly stops operating. Of the following, the FIRST thing that you should do is to
    A. remove the casing of the drill to see whether the insulation of the armature is damaged
    B. check whether the cord is still plugged into the outlet
    C. check the fuses in the supply circuit
    D. inspecft the cord for a broken wire

19. A cold chisel with a "mushroomed" head is properly "dressed" by
    A. filing the cutting edge
    B. heating the head until it is red hot and quenching it in oil
    C. grinding off the turned over material
    D. heating the head of the chisel until it is red hot and, after letting it cool slowly, tapping it until all the chips fall off

20. Of the following sets of items, the BEST one to use to clean and adjust ignition points is
    A. crescent wrench, V-block, and sandpaper
    B. screwdriver, feeler gauge, and point file
    C. scraper, micrometer, and sandpaper
    D. pincers, micrometer, and emery cloth

KEY (CORRECT ANSWERS)

1.	A	11.	B
2.	D	12.	B
3.	A	13.	D
4.	C	14.	B
5.	B	15.	D
6.	B	16.	C
7.	D	17.	A
8.	B	18.	B
9.	A	19.	C
10.	A	20.	B

TEST 3

DIRECTIONS: Each question or incomplete statement is followed by several suggested answers or completions. Select the one that BEST answers the question or completes the statement. *PRINT THE LETTER OF THE CORRECT ANSWER IN THE SPACE AT THE RIGHT.*

1. Assume that, while you are using an electric drill with a long electric cord, the drill suddenly stops operating. Of the following, the FIRST thing that you should do is to
   A. remove the casing of the drill to see whether the insulation of the armature is damaged
   B. check whether the cord is still plugged into the outlet
   C. check the fuses in the supply circuit
   D. inspect the cord for a broken wire

   1.____

2. A cold chisel with a "mushroomed" head is PROPERLY "dressed" by
   A. filing the cutting edge
   B. heating the head until it is red hot and quenching it in oil
   C. grinding off the turned over material
   D. heating the head of the chisel until it is red hot and, after letting it cool slowly, tapping it until all the chips fall off

   2.____

3. A pipe reamer is used to
   A. thread pipe
   B. enlarge the size of a pipe
   C. remove burrs from the inside of a pipe
   D. join pipes of different sizes

   3.____

4. Where only a short swing of the handle is possible, the BEST tool to use to tighten a nut or bolt is the _____ wrench.
   A. Stillson   B. open end   C. monkey   D. ratchet

   4.____

5. The wrench which is used on set screws is COMMONLY called the _____ wrench.
   A. torque   B. Allen   C. Stillson   D. Crescent

   5.____

6. A box wrench is BEST used on
   A. Allen screws   B. pipe fittings
   C. hexagonal nuts   D. knurled thumb screws

   6.____

7. The BEST screwdriver to use when driving screws in close quarters is the
   A. butt   B. angled   C. Phillips   D. offset

   7.____

8. A "12-24" screw is MOST likely a _____ screw.
   A. machine   b. sheet metal   C. lag   D. wood

   8.____

21

9. The one of the following fasteners which is threaded at both ends is the
   A. lag screw   B. stud
   C. bolt   D. machine screw

10. Tips of masonry drills are USUALLY made of
    A. carbide   B. corundum   C. mild steel   D. beryllium

11. A 5-inch length of pipe with male threads at each end is called a
    A. stud   B. coupling   C. sleeve   D. nipple

12. Grade No. 2 sandpaper is
    A. finer than grade 1/0   B. coarser than grade 3
    C. finer than grade 2/0   D. coarser than grade 1

13. The one of the following lists of materials which includes ALL of the ingredients of concrete is cement,
    A. gravel, and water   B. lime, sand, and water
    C. sand, gravel, and water   D. sand, and water

14. The MAIN purpose of the tool known as a file card is to _____ files.
    A. clean   B. sort out
    C. prevent damage to   D. sharpen

15. The pull exerted by a man lifting a 200 lb. load by means of a four-part block and fall, ignoring friction, is _____ lbs.
    A. 100   B. 75   C. 50   D. 25

16. Of the following, turpentine is a solvent for
    A. shellac   B. latex paint
    C. calcimine   D. red lead paint

17. In a truck's gasoline engine, the condenser is a part of the
    A. distributor   B. cooling system
    C. power take off   D. fuel system

18. Pneumatic tools are operated by a(n)
    A. air compressor   B. Pelton wheel
    C. Archimedean screw   D. hydraulic ram

19. The gauge on the tank of an air compressor measures
    A. temperature of air in the tank   B. pressure of air in the tank
    C. humidity of the atmosphere   D. barometric pressure

20. A paint sprayer may have gauges showing the pressure of the tank, the paint pressure, and the atomizer pressure. When the sprayer is operating properly, the
    A. paint pressure is higher than the tank pressure
    B. atomizer pressure is higher than the tank pressure
    C. paint and atomizer pressures are equal
    D. atomizer pressure is higher than the paint pressure

20.____

KEY (CORRECT ANSWERS)

1.	B	11.	D
2.	C	12.	D
3.	C	13.	C
4.	D	14.	A
5.	B	15.	C
6.	C	16.	D
7.	D	17.	A
8.	A	18.	A
9.	B	19.	B
10.	A	20.	D

EXAMINATION SECTION
TEST 1

DIRECTIONS: Each question or incomplete statement is followed by several suggested answers or completions. Select the one that BEST answers the question or completes the statement. *PRINT THE LETTER OF THE CORRECT ANSWER IN THE SPACE AT THE RIGHT.*

1. A traffic sign states that parking is permitted on Sundays and Holidays. According to the traffic regulations of the city, the holiday on which parking is NOT permitted in the area covered by the sign is

    A. New Year's Day
    B. Memorial Day
    C. Thanksgiving Day
    D. Lincoln's Birthday

1._____

2. An intrastate bus is a bus that runs

    A. only in one state
    B. in 2 states only
    C. between the United States and Canada
    D. between any states in the Union

2._____

3. According to the traffic regulations of the Department of Traffic, a pedestrian facing a red signal at an intersection

    A. has the right of way over automobiles having a green signal
    B. has the right of way over trucks having a green signal
    C. may not enter the intersection facing the red signal
    D. may enter the intersection, facing the red signal, if he can do so safely without interfering with traffic

3._____

4. This sentence was taken from the traffic regulations of the City Department of Traffic with respect to yield signs:
Proceeding past such sign with resultant collision or other impedance or interference with traffic on the intersecting street shall be deemed prima facie in violation of this regulation. The words prima facie mean MOST NEARLY

    A. probably
    B. possibly or likely
    C. literally or completely
    D. guilty

4._____

5. Where signs on city streets do not indicate otherwise, the MAXIMUM speed limit in the city is, in miles per hour,

    A. 15   B. 20   C. 25   D. 30

5._____

6. Making a U-turn in the city is NOT permissible on any

    A. street
    B. street in a residential district
    C. street in a business district
    D. 2-way street

6._____

7. A person stops his car in front of a hydrant and remains in the car. According to the traffic regulations of the City Department of Traffic,

7._____

A. this is illegal if he is within 15 feet of the hydrant
B. it is legal
C. he does not have to move if so ordered by a policeman
D. he may remain there provided he is far enough away from the hydrant so as not to interfere with hose lines

8. Taxicabs are

   A. not permitted to cruise
   B. permitted to cruise in residential areas only
   C. permitted to cruise in business areas only
   D. permitted to cruise in all boroughs except Manhattan

9. Of the following, the one that is the MAIN cause of fatal accidents is

   A. direction signals not working
   B. windshield wipers not working
   C. improper alignment of the wheels
   D. defective brakes

10. The capacity of an approach to an intersection is prinarily dependent upon

    A. slope of through band
    B. cycle length
    C. offsets
    D. through band width

11. To handle heavy traffic movements which tend to cause congestion at an intersection, it is often necessary to

    A. use a standard 3-color (RAG) traffic control signal on all four corners
    B. add arrow indications to traffic signals permitting movements in a certain direction when other traffic is halted
    C. use 2-color instead of 3-color traffic signals
    D. install a flasher caution signal facing the direction of heavy traffic flow

12. Elm Street and Oak Street are one-way streets that intersect.

    A. Cars may turn either right from both streets or left from both streets depending on the direction of travel.
    B. If cars may turn right into one street, they may not turn right into the other.
    C. Only right turns are permitted in both streets.
    D. Only left turns are permitted in both streets.

13. Of the following intersections where one street dead ends into another, the one that is SAFEST is

C. [diagram with 45°]   D. [diagram with 30°]

14. Driver interview, tag on vehicle, and postal cards are all methods of obtaining information relative to

    A. vehicle miles traveled
    B. accident data
    C. motor vehicle registration
    D. origin and destination

15. A study of motor vehicle volume normally includes all but one of the following:

    A. Directional movements
    B. Motor vehicle occupancy
    C. Motor vehicle classification
    D. Number of vehicles per unit of time

16. Counts made with automatic recorders must always be supplemented with manual observations to ascertain

    A. hourly distribution
    B. directional distribution
    C. vehicle classification
    D. turning movements

17. A cordon count is USUALLY made on a

    A. weekday   B. Saturday   C. Sunday   D. holiday

18. Of the following vehicles, the one that need NOT be stopped at an origin and destination station is a

    A. bus
    B. foreign car
    C. station wagon
    D. coal truck

19. A turning movement count is USUALLY taken at

    A. a toll station
    B. a highway intersection
    C. a bus terminal
    D. the end of a highway

20. A manual traffic count is

    A. a mechanical counter tabulating pedestrians
    B. the number of manuals issued in a traffic survey
    C. an estimated volume of traffic
    D. the number of motor vehicles counted by the person assigned

21. Traffic counts that are made within the city limits are _____ counts.   21.____

    A. rural   B. suburban
    C. urban   D. sample

22. When questioning a driver in a traffic survey, the interviewer should   22.____

    A. explain briefly the reason for the interview
    B. insist on having his questions answered
    C. get the signature of the person interviewed
    D. report the person interviewed, if he did not cooperate

23. In gathering data for a traffic survey, it was decided to use only the period from 6:00 A.M.   23.____
    to 10:00 P.M.
    The reason for choosing this period is MOST likely that

    A. employee morale would drop if the inspectors were required to work during the night
    B. the public would not cooperate during the late night or early morning hours
    C. it is inconsiderate to disturb the public in the middle of the night
    D. the information obtained at that time would be considered adequate

24. Of the following data, the one that is MOST significant in a traffic survey is the   24.____

    A. locations between which the car travels
    B. number of cars in the driver's family
    C. number of drivers operating the car
    D. average annual mileage of the car

25. The MAIN purpose for making a motor vehicle volume survey of a particular route is to   25.____
    provide basic data for determining

    A. the extent of group riding
    B. whether prevailing speeds are too fast for conditions
    C. a plan of traffic control
    D. where and how much parking space may be needed

26. Of the following studies, the one which is LEAST related and would probably NOT be   26.____
    included in making a traffic safety survey is

    A. street and off-street parking
    B. driver observance of stop signs
    C. pedestrian observance of traffic signals
    D. accident records and facts

27. Of the following, the one which would NOT usually require a traffic survey is   27.____

    A. revision of parking time limits to assure most efficient usage of curb space
    B. creation of off-street parking facilities
    C. important trends in traffic characteristics and transportation demands
    D. complaints from residents in a particular area on the disturbance caused by heavy traffic moving through that area

28. A *spot-map* is a graphic method which is used to

    A. show types of traffic signals located at the main intersections in a community
    B. analyze the distribution of accidents within a community area
    C. arrive at reasonable accident rates
    D. show grades, width, roadway surface, and merging traffic streams in a community

29. A survey was made for the purposes of installing traffic control signals at a certain intersection of a main street and cross street in a certain area. The survey shows that although traffic is relatively heavy during the day, it becomes very light at night.
    In such a situation, it would be MOST desirable to

    A. continue the full sequence of indications as in the daytime
    B. continue operation of the signals, but lengthen the cycle of intervals
    C. completely extinguish the signals leaving the intersection uncontrolled
    D. extinguish the signals but provide a flasher mechanism on the controller

30. If the capacity of an approach to an intersection is 3600 vehicles per hour of green and the go phase on this approach is 40 seconds out of a 60-second cycle, the equivalent volume is _____ vehicles per hour.

    A. 2400   B. 3600   C. 5400   D. 2000

31. If a section of a highway 10 miles long carries an annual daily traffic of 5,000 vehicles and there are two deaths in a year, the death rate is

    A. 2.0 deaths per 5,000 vehicles
    B. 11.0 deaths per 100 million vehicle miles
    C. 11.0 deaths per million vehicle miles
    D. 2.0 deaths per 50,000 vehicle miles

32. If the difference in elevation between two intersections 300 feet apart is 6 feet, the grade along the street is

    A. 2%   B. 2   C. 0.002   D. 6%

33. If on a highway a car passes a given point every 5 seconds, the number of cars per hour passing the given point on the highway is

    A. 360   B. 480   C. 600   D. 720

34. The cost of concrete paving for a strip of driveway 50 feet long, 10 feet wide, and 6 inches deep, if concrete in place costs $30 per cubic yard, is, in dollars, MOST NEARLY
    (27 cubic feet = 1 cubic yard)

    A. 278   B. 318   C. 329   D. 380

Questions 35-38.

DIRECTIONS: Questions 35 through 38 relate to the sketch below.

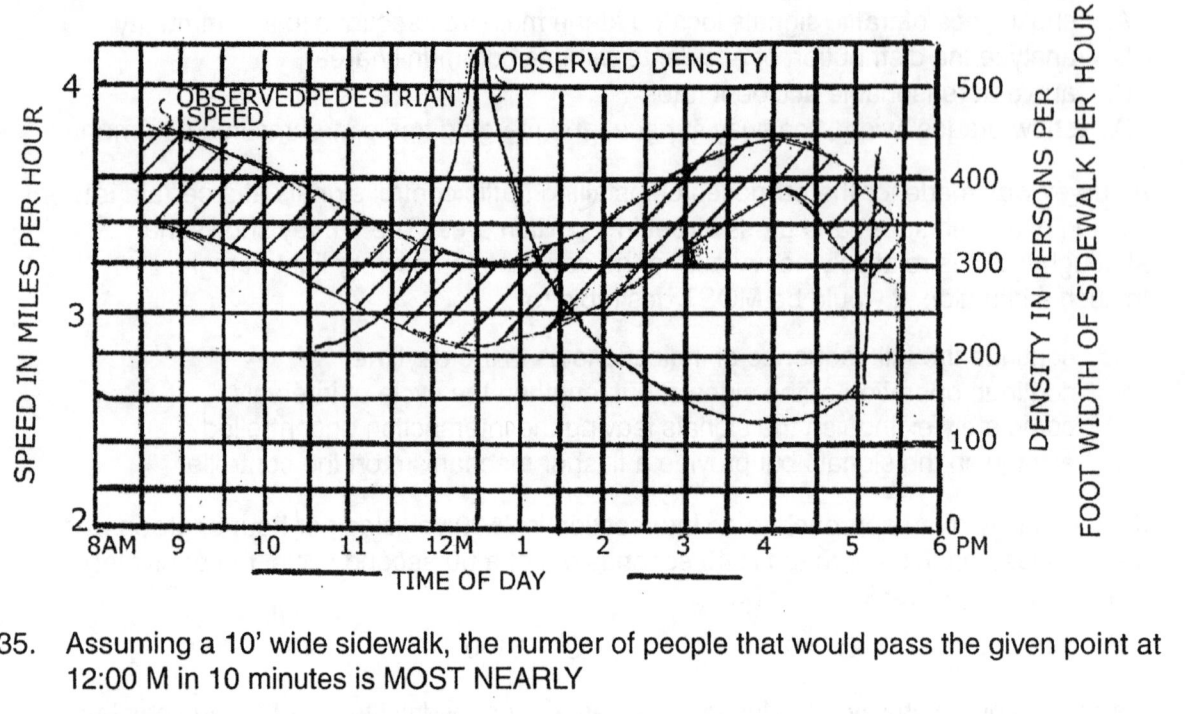

35. Assuming a 10' wide sidewalk, the number of people that would pass the given point at 12:00 M in 10 minutes is MOST NEARLY

    A. 580 B. 680 C. 780 D. 880

36. At 10:00 A.M., you could expect a person to be walking at a speed

    A. of 3 miles per hour
    B. between 300 and 420 feet per hour
    C. between 3.2 and 3.65 miles per hour
    D. of 4.5 feet per second

37. The highest average number of people using the sidewalk will USUALLY occur at

    A. 9 A.M. B. 12:30 P.M. C. 4 P.M. D. 5 P.M.

38. Of the following statements relating to the diagram, the one that is MOST NEARLY CORRECT is

    A. the minimum walking speed observed is 2 miles per hour
    B. data for the survey was taken continuously for 24 hours
    C. as the number of people using the sidewalk increases, the speed at which they walk decreases
    D. the minimum observed density is 300 people per hour per foot width of sidewalk

39. A vehicle moving at 30 miles per hour is moving at a speed, in feet per second, MOST NEARLY

    A. 30 B. 44 C. 52 D. 60

40. A street map is to a scale 1 inch equals 600 feet. A distance of 1/2 inch on the drawing represents a distance on the ground, in feet, MOST NEARLY

    A. 300 B. 600 C. 900 D. 1,200

Questions 41-42.

DIRECTIONS: Questions 41 and 42 refer to the sketches below.

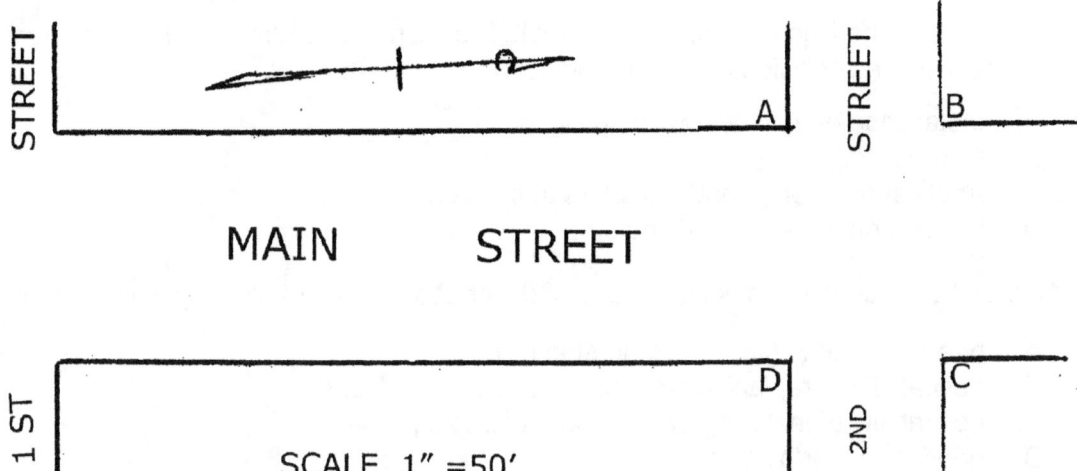

41. The length of block from 1st Street to 2nd Street is MOST NEARLY   41._____

    A. 150'   B. 250'   C. 350'   D. 450'

42. The northeast corner of Main and 2nd is   42._____

    A. A   B. B   C. C   D. D

43. The sketch shown at the right shows a right triangular island at the intersection of three streets on which is installed traffic signals A and B. Traffic conditions have increased and require than an additional traffic light be installed at point C. Electric power for signal C is to be taken from the junction box located at the base of post A and extended to C as shown by the broken line.
With the distances given as shown, the length of conduit, in feet, required to extend power from A to C is MOST NEARLY   43._____

    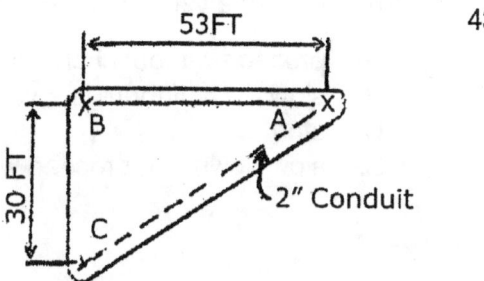

    A. 44   B. 60   C. 83   D. 75

44. The volume of traffic at a certain location increased frori 1,000 to 1,500 vehicles per hour. The percentage increase of traffic is MOST NEARLY   44._____

    A. 33%   B. 50%   C. 60%   D. 40%

45. A collision diagram would MOST likely NOT show   45._____

    A. direction of movement of each vehicle or pedestrian involved
    B. distance of the accident to the nearest building line
    C. date and hour of the accident
    D. weather and road conditions

46. A graphical representation of the detailed nature of accidents occurring at a location is known as a

   A. collision diagram
   B. condition diagram
   C. accident summary
   D. accident spot map

47. Which one of the following remedies is MOST appropriate to eliminate high accident frequency involving collisions with fixed objects?

   A. Installation of advance warning signs
   B. Reroute traffic
   C. Application of paint and reflectors to fixed object
   D. Installation of center dividing strip

48. One of the reasons for making a study of driver observance of stop signs is to study the

   A. need for retaining or removing stop signs
   B. desirability of replacing stop sign with a police officer
   C. desirability of installing pedestrian crosswalk lines
   D. need for speed zoning

49. Which one of the following remedies is MOST appropriate to eliminate high accident frequency involving pedestrian-vehicular collisions at intersections?

   A. Installation of turning guide lines
   B. Installation of painted pavement lane lines
   C. Installation of pedestrian cross-walk lines
   D. Removal of view obstruction

50. The driver of a vehicle approaching a yield sign is required to

   A. proceed without changing speed
   B. slow down if there is a vehicle in the intersection
   C. stop
   D. slow down and proceed with caution

KEY (CORRECT ANSWERS)

1. D	11. B	21. C	31. B	41. B
2. A	12. B	22. A	32. A	42. C
3. C	13. A	23. D	33. D	43. B
4. C	14. D	24. A	34. A	44. B
5. C	15. B	25. C	35. A	45. B
6. C	16. C	26. A	36. C	46. A
7. A	17. A	27. D	37. B	47. C
8. A	18. A	28. B	38. C	48. A
9. D	19. B	29. D	39. B	49. C
10. D	20. D	30. A	40. A	50. D

TEST 2

DIRECTIONS: Each question or incomplete statement is followed by several suggested answers or completions. Select the one that BEST answers the question or completes the statement. *PRINT THE LETTER OF THE CORRECT ANSWER IN THE SPACE AT THE RIGHT.*

1. No person shall stop, stand, or park a vehicle closer to a fire hydrant than

    A. 17'   B. 10'   C. 15'   D. 12'

2. When stopping is prohibited by signs or regulations and no conflict exists with other traffic, the driver of a vehicle is

    A. permitted to stop temporarily
    B. not permitted to stop
    C. permitted to stand
    D. permitted to park

3. Where there is a *No Parking* sign, a person may

    A. not stop his vehicle
    B. stop his vehicle to discharge passengers
    C. stop his vehicle and leave it unattended for a maximum of 10 minutes
    D. stop his vehicle and leave it unattended for a maximum of 5 minutes

4. Of the following, the MOST restrictive parking sign is

    A. no standing   B. no parking
    C. taxi stand   D. bus stop

5. A highway sign that is classified as a Guide sign is

    A. Stop   B. No Passing
    C. Narrow Road   D. North Bound

6. A highway sign that is classified as a Warning sign is

    A. No U Turn   B. Hill
    C. Speed Limit 50   D. Do Not Enter

7. A highway sign that is classified as a Regulatory sign is

    A. One Way   B. Men Working
    C. RR   D. Detour

8. A traffic device that has the same effect as a stop sign is a

    A. flashing yellow   B. flashing red
    C. yield sign   D. detour sign

9. A warrant for a certain type of traffic control device is a(n)

    A. official order to install the device
    B. application from a local community for the device
    C. reason for installing the device
    D. request to remove the device

10. Shapes of signs on state highways convey definite information. The sign to the right means
    A. steep hill - slow down
    B. come to a full stop
    C. you may proceed with caution
    D. approaching narrow bridge

11. Where flasher mechanisms must be installed at intersections of a main street and a cross street as a warning signal, it would be BEST to have flashing
    A. amber on the main street and flashing red on the cross street
    B. red on the main street and flashing amber on the cross street
    C. red on the main street only
    D. amber on the cross street only

12. The primary purpose of *progressive timing* of traffic control signals is to
    A. allow the largest volume of traffic flow at the safest speed along a particular route
    B. permit slow drivers to travel at an increased speed
    C. permit the largest volume of pedestrian traffic to cross safely at the same time
    D. reduce traveling speed so that motorists have vehicles under constant control

13. A hazard marker, for example, at the end of a dead-end street, would MOST likely be
    A. yellow background with black letters
    B. yellow background with red letters
    C. a reflector type marker
    D. a warning sign

14. Of the following, the BEST reason for having markings that are uniform in design, position, and application is that
    A. less skill is required to provide the markings
    B. they cost less when they are uniform
    C. there is no harm done in providing them even where there is no need
    D. they may be recognized and understood instantly

15. If numerous pedestrian accidents occur at a signalized intersection, a pertinent study to help evaluate the problem would be
    A. signal timing
    B. motor vehicle volume
    C. pedestrian observance of traffic signals
    D. driver observance of pedestrian right of way

16. Which one of the following types of fixed-time signal systems is MOST desirable? _____ system.
    A. Flexible progressive   B. Alternate
    C. Simple progressive   D. Simultaneous

17. Of the following statements relating to traffic actuated signals, the one that is CORRECT is

    A. it is especially useful at little used intersections
    B. the length of time the green light is on is not constant
    C. it can only be used at the intersection of one-way streets
    D. it can only be used at the intersection of two-way streets

18. An advantage of the three lens signal (red, yellow, and green) over the two lens signal (red and green) is that it

    A. enables cars within the intersection to clear
    B. allows pedestrians to cross the intersection safely
    C. may be operated as a traffic actuated signal
    D. may be used as a caution signal when not used as a stop and go signal

19. A fixed time signal is one by which traffic stops and goes

    A. for equal time periods
    B. according to a predetermined time schedule
    C. by manual control
    D. according to the volume of traffic

20. The proper installation of vehicle detectors is MOST important for a

    A. pedestrian push-button installation
    B. fixed time signal system
    C. traffic actuated signal
    D. progressive system

21. Of the following, the one that is NOT considered a disadvantage in the use of pavement markings is they

    A. may be obliterated by snow
    B. may not be clearly visible when wet
    C. must be used with other devices such as traffic signs or signals
    D. are subject to traffic wear

22. *It is often desirable to mark lines on the pavement to indicate the limits and the clearance of the overhang on turning streetcars.*
    This safety measure is NOT required in this city because

    A. there are no streetcars in this city
    B. city traffic is controlled by other suitable devices
    C. city traffic is not fast enough to require it
    D. streetcars in this city turn only at the depot and not in the streets

23. A yellow curb marking may be used at all but one of the following:

    A. A fire hydrant
    B. A bus stop
    C. A depressed curb leading to a loading platform
    D. Where parking is prohibited from 8 A.M. to 6 P.M.

24. Stop lines or limit lines are used to indicate

   A. parking space limits to prevent encroachment on a fire hydrant zone
   B. the marking of stalls where parking meters are used
   C. the point behind which vehicles must stop in compliance with a traffic signal
   D. where pedestrians are permitted to cross a street

25. An island, as applied to traffic control,

   A. provides a safe area for a traffic patrolman
   B. segregates pedestrians and vehicles
   C. provides a clear area for a bus stop
   D. establishes a barrier between opposite lanes of traffic

26. Of the following, the one which is NOT a method for providing channelization of traffic is by

   A. permanent islands or strips
   B. pavement markings
   C. use of stanchions
   D. mounting traffic signal at center of intersection

27. The PRIMARY purpose for marking the pavement of heavily traveled thoroughfares into lanes is to

   A. slow up traffic
   B. prevent accidents
   C. speed up traffic
   D. keep slow drivers on the right side of the road

28. When parking is not otherwise restricted in the city, no person shall park a commercial vehicle in excess of ____ hours.

   A. 2   B. 4   C. 3   D. 6

29. A condition which need NOT be considered in making a general parking survey is

   A. reasons for parking at various locations
   B. street and roadway widths and surfaces
   C. average time vehicles remained at various locations
   D. sidewalk obstructions, such as lamp posts and fire posts

30. Concerning the purpose of parking meters, the statement which is NOT true is

   A. assist in reducing overtime parking at the curb
   B. increase parking turnover
   C. eliminate the need for off-street parking facilities
   D. facilitate enforcement of parking regulations

31. The MOST efficient layout of parking spaces in a large lot is to place the stalls ____ to the aisles.

   A. parallel   B. at right angles
   C. at a 30° angle   D. at a 60° angle

32. The time limits set by cities for parking on city streets during the daytime   32.____

   A. is considered strictly a policing problem
   B. is shorter in concentrated business areas
   C. will vary directly with the amount of traffic on the street
   D. is uniform for all sections of the city

33. Four parts of a survey report are listed below, not necessarily in their proper order: 33.____

   I. Body of report
   II. Synopsis of report
   III. Letter of transmittal
   IV. Conclusions

   Which one of the following represents the BEST sequence for inclusion of these parts in a report?

   A. III, IV, I, II
   C. III, II, I, IV
   B. II, I, III, IV
   D. I, III, IV, II

34. A traffic control inspector recommends that an illuminated advertising sign near a signal light be removed.   34.____
   The reason for this recommendation is MOST likely that

   A. a driver's attention may be attracted to the sign rather than the road
   B. the similarity of colors may cause confusion
   C. such signs mar the beauty of the roadside
   D. the sign encroaches upon public property

35. Of the following, the MOST important value of a good report is that it   35.____

   A. reflects credit upon the person who submitted the report
   B. provides good reference material
   C. expedites official business
   D. expresses the need for official action

36. The MOST important requirement in report writing is   36.____

   A. promptness in turning in reports
   B. length
   C. grammatical construction
   D. accuracy

37. You have discovered an error in your report submitted to the main office.   37.____
   You should

   A. wait until the error is discovered in the main office and then correct it
   B. go directly to the supervisor in the main office after working hours and ask him unofficially to correct the answer
   C. notify the main office immediately so that the error can be corrected if necessary
   D. do nothing, since it is possible that one error will have little effect on the total report

38. The use of *radar* by police as a means of apprehending motorists who exceed the speed limit has recently been challenged in court on the grounds that   38.____

   A. the motorists are not forewarned
   B. the speed limits have not been posted

C. the equipment does not give reliable results
D. there is no sworn evidence that a speed violation took place

39. Of the following, the one which is generally classified as a commercial vehicle is a

   A. station wagon
   B. chauffeur-driven passenger car
   C. taxicab
   D. truck

40. A divided arterial highway for through traffic with full or partial control of access is generally referred to as an

   A. expressway   B. parkway
   C. freeway   D. major street

41. Of the following, the MOST important advantage to be gained by converting a two-way north-south street to a one-way street is

   A. *decrease* the number of accidents
   B. *decrease* the need for bus service
   C. *increase* the average speed of traffic
   D. *increase* the turnover at curbs

42. Of the following, the BEST road for heavy traffic is

   A. two lane   B. three lane
   C. four lane undivided D. four lane divided

43. When weekend traffic differs greatly from weekday traffic,

   A. the average daily traffic figure is used in estimating weekend traffic
   B. weekend traffic counts should be made as well as weekday counts
   C. the traffic count for another road in the area should be used
   D. traffic counts should be made at different seasons of the year

44. Work is now going on to approximately double the car-carrying capacity of which one of the following?

   A. Car parkways   B. Bridges
   C. Tunnels   D. HOV lanes

45. The MOST recent major change in the specifications of the federally aided highway program is

   A. increasing the permissible grades or roads
   B. requirements for drainage
   C. lane width
   D. vertical clearance under bridges

46. A recent newspaper article reported that small cars are considered a danger to the federally aided highway program.
    Of the following, the one that may be considered as the reason for this danger is

A. they consume less gas providing less taxes for the highway program
B. the lanes of the new highways are too wide for these cars, disorganizing the traffic flow pattern
C. the two-car family is upsetting the estimates of traffic flow
D. foreign cars are hurting American business

47. Span-wire mountings of fixed traffic control signals is generally

   A. used in the city at heavily traveled intersections
   B. used in the city at intersections in isolated areas
   C. not used in the city
   D. used at locations where more than two streets intersect

48. A map depicting straight lines drawn from points of vehicle origin to points of vehicle destination is known as _____ map.

   A. desire line   B. traffic flow
   C. bar   D. pie

49. Brake reaction time for most people is APPROXIMATELY _____ seconds.

   A. 0.6   B. 2.0   C. 0.1   D. 1.4

50. Trucks should travel along prescribed truck routes if their overall length is equal to or exceeds

   A. 27'   B. 41'   C. 30'   D. 33'

KEY (CORRECT ANSWERS)

1. C	11. A	21. C	31. B	41. C
2. B	12. A	22. A	32. B	42. D
3. B	13. C	23. D	33. C	43. B
4. A	14. D	24. C	34. B	44. D
5. D	15. C	25. B	35. C	45. D
6. B	16. A	26. D	36. D	46. A
7. A	17. B	27. C	37. C	47. C
8. B	18. D	28. C	38. C	48. A
9. C	19. B	29. D	39. D	49. A
10. B	20. C	30. C	40. A	50. D

EXAMINATION SECTION
TEST 1

DIRECTIONS: Each question or incomplete statement is followed by several suggested answers or completions. Select the one that BEST answers the question or completes the statement. *PRINT THE LETTER OF THE CORRECT ANSWER IN THE SPACE AT THE RIGHT.*

1. A set of conductors originating at the load side of the service equipment and supplying the main and/or one or more secondary distribution centers is commonly called a
    A. circuit   B. line   C. cable   D. feeder

    1.____

2. A 5-microfarad condenser is charged by putting 100 volts d.c. across its terminals. If this condenser is now placed across another condenser which has the same capacity rating and is identical in every other respect, the NEW voltage across these two condensers is *most nearly*
    A. 100   B. 75   C. 50   D. 25

    2.____

3. A synchronous condenser, so far as construction and appearance is concerned, *closely* resembles a(n)
    A. electrolytic condenser   B. synchronous motor
    C. synchroscope   D. wound rotor induction motor

    3.____

4. In an electric spot welding machine, the primary winding contains 200 turns of #10 wire and the secondary contains one turn made up of laminated copper sheeting.
    When the primary current is 5 amperes, the current, in amperes, passing through the metal to be welded is *approximately*
    A. 100   B. 200   C. 500   D. 1000

    4.____

5. With reference to an electric spot welding machine, the metal BEST suited to be united by spot welding is
    A. copper   B. zinc   C. lead   D. iron

    5.____

6. Two steel bars "G" and "H" have equal dimensions but one of them is a magnet and the other an ordinary piece of soft steel. In order to find out which one of the two bars is the magnet, you would touch the point midway between the ends of bar "G" with one end of bar "H". Then, if bar "H" tends to
    A. *pull* bar "G," bar "H" is not the magnet
    B. *pull* bar "G," bar "H" is the magnet
    C. *repel* bar "G," bar "H" is the magnet
    D. *repel* bar "G," bar "H" is not the magnet

    6.____

7. The MAIN purpose of a cutting fluid used in threading electrical conduits is to
    A. prevent the formation of electrolytic pockets
    B. improve the finish of the thread
    C. wash away the chips
    D. prevent the eventual formation of rust

8. If a certain electrical job requires 212 feet of ½" rigid conduit, the number of lengths that you should requisition is
    A. 16   B. 18   C. 20   D. 22

9. The number of threads per inch *commonly* used for ½" electrical conduit is
    A. 15   B. 14   C. 13   D. 12

10. For mounting a heavy pull box on a hollow tile wall, it is BEST to use
    A. lag screws   B. masonry nails
    C. toggle bolts   D. expansion shields

11. For mounting an outlet box on a concrete ceiling, it is BEST to use
    A. ordinary wood screws   B. masonry nails
    C. expansion screw anchors   D. toggle bolts

12. The electrical code states that incandescent lamps shall not be equipped with medium bases if above 1500 watts; special approved bases or other devices shall be used.
    In accordance with the above statement, the lamp base that you should use for a 750 watt incandescent lamp is the _____ base.
    A. medium   B. candelabra   C. intermediate   D. mogul

13. In order to remove rough edges after cutting, all ends of conduit should be
    A. filed   B. sanded   C. reamed   D. honed

14. Where a conduit enters a box, in order to protect the wire from abrasion, you should use an approved
    A. coupling   B. close nipple   C. locknut   D. bushing

15. The MAXIMUM number of No. 10 type R conductors permitted in a ¾" conduit is
    A. 8   B. 6   C. 4   D. 2

16. A large switch which opens automatically when the current *exceeds* a predetermined limit is called a
    A. disconnect   B. contactor
    C. circuit breaker   D. limit switch

17. The flux *commonly* used for soldering electrical wires is
    A. rosin   B. borax   C. zinc chloride   D. tallow

18. The cost of the electrical energy consumed by a 50-watt lamp burning for 100 hours as compared to that consumed by a 100-watt lamp burning for 50 hours is
    A. four times as much
    B. three times as much
    C. twice as much
    D. the same

18._____

19. Pneumatic tools are run by
    A. electricity
    B. steam
    C. compressed air
    D. oil

19._____

20. It is required to make a right angle turn in a conduit run in which there are already 3 quarter bends following the last pull box. The fitting BEST suited to *properly* do this is a(n)
    A. cross
    B. tee
    C. union
    D. ell

20._____

21. A 10,000 ohms resistance in an electronic timing switch burned out and must be replaced. The service manual states that this resistance should have an accuracy of 5%. This means that the value of the new resistance should differ from 10,000 ohms by NOT more than _____ ohms.
    A. 50
    B. 150
    C. 300
    D. 500

21._____

22. Of the following, the A.W.G. size of single conductor bare copper wire which has the LOWEST resistance per foot is
    A. #40
    B. #10
    C. #00
    D. #0

22._____

23. The voltage output of 6 ordinary flashlight dry cells of the zinc-carbon type, when connected in parallel with each other, will be *approximately* _____ volts.
    A. 1.5
    B. 3
    C. 9
    D. 12

23._____

24. Full load current for a 5-ohm, 20-watt resistor is
    A. 4
    B. 3
    C. 2
    D. 1

24._____

25. An auto-transformer could NOT be used to
    A. step-up voltage
    B. step-down voltage
    C. act as a choke cell
    D. change a.c. frequency

25._____

KEY (CORRECT ANSWERS)

1.	D	11.	C
2.	C	12.	D
3.	B	13.	C
4.	D	14.	D
5.	D	15.	C
6.	B	16.	C
7.	B	17.	A
8.	D	18.	D
9.	B	19.	C
10.	C	20.	D

21. D
22. C
23. A
24. C
25. D

TEST 2

DIRECTIONS: Each question or incomplete statement is followed by several suggested answers or completions. Select the one that BEST answers the question or completes the statement. *PRINT THE LETTER OF THE CORRECT ANSWER IN THE SPACE AT THE RIGHT.*

1. A resistor is connected across a supply of "E" volts. The heat produced in this resistor is proportion to I^2R. If R is reduced in value, the heat produced in this resistor now
   A. increases
   B. decreases
   C. remains the same
   D. is indeterminate

   1.____

2. A d.c. shunt generator has developed some trouble. You find that there is an open armature coil. As a *temporary* measure, you should
   A. use new brushes having a thickness of at least 3 commutator segments
   B. bridge the two commutator bars across which the open coil is connected
   C. use new brushes having a thickness of at least 4 commutator segments
   D. disconnect the open coil from the commutator

   2.____

3. A cable composed of two insulated stranded conductors laid parallel, having a common cover is called a _____ cable.
   A. twin
   B. duplex
   C. concentric
   D. sector

   3.____

4. If two equal resistance coils are connected in parallel, the resistance of this combination is *equal* to
   A. the resistance of one coil
   B. ½ the resistance of one coil
   C. twice the resistance of one coil
   D. ¼ the resistance of one coil

   4.____

5. A condenser whose capacity is one microfarad is connected in parallel with a condenser whose capacity is 2 microfarads. This combination is equal to a single condenser having a capacity, in microfarads, of *approximately*
   A. 2/3
   B. 1
   C. 3
   D. 3/2

   5.____

Questions 6-7.

DIRECTIONS: Questions 6 and 7 are to be answered on the basis of the diagram sketched below.

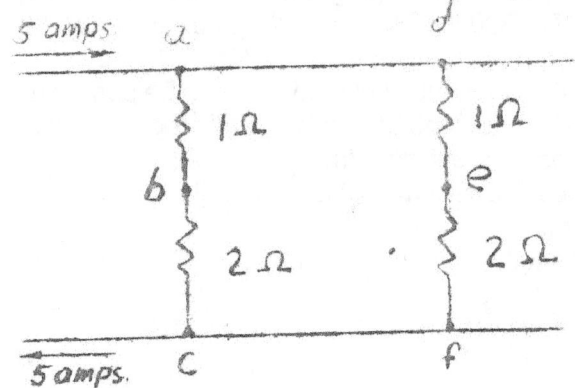

45

6. With reference to the diagram above, the current flowing through resistance ab is _____ amperes.
   A. 5   B. 4   C. 2½   D. 1½

7. With reference to the diagram above, the voltage difference between points b and e is _____ volt(s).
   A. 1   B. 10   C. 5   D. 0

8. The resistance of copper wire is _____ proportional to its _____.
   A. directly; cross-sectional area
   B. directly; length
   C. inversely; length
   D. inversely; diameter

9. The insulation resistance of 50 ft. of #12 BS rubber-covered wire, as compared to the insulation resistance of 100 ft. of this wire, is
   A. one-half as much
   B. the same
   C. four times as much
   D. twice as much

10. The resistance of a 150-scale voltmeter is 10,000 ohms. The power, in watts, consumed by this voltmeter when it is connected across a 100-volt circuit is
    A. 10   B. 5   C. 2.5   D. 1

11. A battery cell having an e.m.f. of 2.2 volts and an internal resistance of 0.2 ohm is connected to an external resistance 0.2 ohm. The current, in amperes, of the battery under this condition is *approximately*
    A. 15   B. 10   C. 2.5   D. 1

12. In reference to the preceding question, the efficiency, in percent, of the battery under this condition is *most nearly*
    A. 70   B. 80   C. 90   D. 100

13. During discharge, the internal resistance of a storage battery
    A. increases
    B. remains the same
    C. decreases
    D. is negative

14. The weight of a round copper bar is given by the formula, 3.14 R^2LK, where R is the radius, L is the length, and K for copper is .32 lbs. per cubic inch. The weight of a round copper bar 8'4" long and 2" in diameter is *approximately*
    A. 400 lbs.   B. 300 lbs.   C. 100 lbs.   D. 50 lbs.

15. Compound d.c. generators are usually wound so as to be somewhat over-compounded. The degree of compounding is *usually* regulated by
    A. shunting more or less current from the series field
    B. shunting more or less current from the shunt field
    C. connecting it short-shunt
    D. connecting it long-shunt

16. With reference to a shunt wound d.c. generator, if the resistance of the field is increased to a value exceeding its critical field resistance, the generator
    A. output may exceed its name plate rating
    B. may burn out when loaded to its name plate rating
    C. output voltage will be less than its name plate rating
    D. cannot build up

16.____

17. The PROPER way to reverse the direction of rotation of a compound motor is to interchange the
    A. line leads
    B. armature connections
    C. shunt-field connections
    D. series field connections

17.____

18. In the d.c. series motor, the field
    A. has comparatively few turns of wire
    B. has comparatively many turns of wire
    C. is connected across the armature
    D. current is less than the line current

18.____

19. In the d.c. series motor, when the load torque is *decreased*, the
    A. armature rotates at a lower speed
    B. armature rotates at a higher speed
    C. current through the field is increased
    D. current through the armature is increased

19.____

20. To fasten an outlet box to a concrete ceiling, you should use
    A. wooden plugs
    B. toggle bolts
    C. mollys
    D. expansion bolts

20.____

21. To fasten an outlet box to a finished hollow tile wall, it is BEST to use
    A. wooden plugs
    B. toggle bolts
    C. through bolts and fishplates
    D. expansion bolts

21.____

Questions 22-23.

DIRECTIONS: Questions 22 and 23 are to be answered in keeping with the statement below and Figure I, which is an incomplete diagram of the connections of a fluorescent lamp. The ballast and starter are not shown.

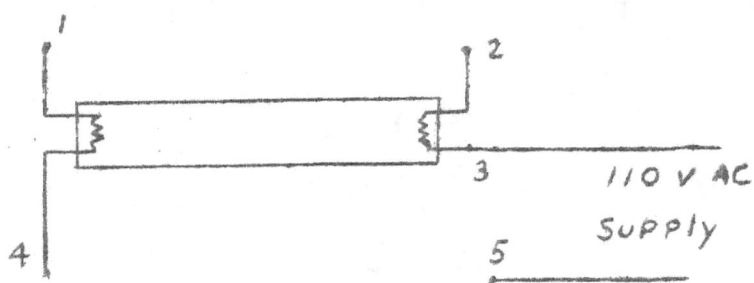

Figure I

The glow type starter used to operate a fluorescent lamp is designed to act as a time switch which will connect the two filament type electrodes in each end of the lamp in series with the ballast during the short preheating period when the lamp is first turned on. The starter will then open the circuit to establish the arc.

22. From the above statement, the competent electrician should know that the starter should be shown connected between points
    A. 4 and 3   B. 1 and 2   C. 4 and 5   D. 3 and 5

23. From the above statement, the competent electrician should know that the choke of the ballast should be shown connected between points
    A. 4 and 3   B. 1 and 2   C. 4 and 5   D. 3 and 5

24. A 6000-watt 3-phase heater composed of three resistance units in delta is connected to a 3-phase, 208-volt supply. The resistance, in ohms, of each resistance unit is *most nearly*
    A. 20.8   B. 41.6   C. 83.2   D. 208

25. Based upon the data given in the preceding question, if the 3-heater resistance units are now connected in star (or wye) to a 3-phase, 208-volt supply, the power, in watts, consumed by this heater is *most nearly*
    A. 10,400   B. 6,000   C. 3,500   D. 2,000

KEY (CORRECT ANSWERS)

1. A   11. B
2. B   12. C
3. A   13. A
4. B   14. C
5. C   15. A

6. C   16. D
7. D   17. B
8. B   18. A
9. D   19. B
10. D   20. D

21. B
22. B
23. C
24. A
25. D

TEST 3

DIRECTIONS: Each question or incomplete statement is followed by several suggested answers or completions. Select the one that BEST answers the question or completes the statement. *PRINT THE LETTER OF THE CORRECT ANSWER IN THE SPACE AT THE RIGHT.*

Questions 1-3.

DIRECTIONS: Questions 1 through 3 are to be answered on the basis of the diagram below. The sketch is a lamp independently controlled from 3 points.

1. The conductor running from the supply to switch No. 1 should be the _____ wire. 1.____
   A. blue   B. white   C. black   D. ground

2. Switch No. 1 should be a _____ switch. 2.____
   A. single-pole   B. four-way   C. two-way   D. three-way

3. Switch No. 2 should be a _____ switch. 3.____
   A. single-pole   B. two-way   C. four-way   D. three-way

Questions 4-15.

DIRECTIONS: Questions 4 through 15 refer to the material given on the next page. Column I lists descriptions of work to be done. Column II lists a tool or instrument for each description listed in Column I. For each description in Column I, select the instrument or tool from Column II which is used for the particular job and write the letter which appears in front of the name of the tool or instrument.

	Column I	Column II	

4. Testing an armature for a shorted coil
5. Measure of electrical pressure
6. Measurement of electrical energy
7. Measurement of electrical power
8. Direct measurement of electrical insulation resistance
9. Direct measurement of electrical resistance (1 ohm to 10,000 ohms)
10. Direct measurement of electrical current
11. Testing to find if supply is d.c. or a.c.
12. Testing the electrolyte of battery
13. Cutting an iron bar
14. Soldering a rat-tail splice
15. A standard for checking the size of wire

A. Neon light
B. Growler
C. Iron-vane Voltmeter
D. Ohmmeter
E. Wattmeter
F. Hot-wire Ammeter
G. Megger
H. Watthour Meter
J. Manometer
K. Cable clamp pliers
L. Pair of test lamps
M. Hack Saw
N. Hydrometer
O. Electrician's blow torch
P. American wire gage
Q. Micrometer
R. Hygrometer
S. Rip Saw

4.____
5.____
6.____
7.____
8.____
9.____
10.____
11.____
12.____
13.____
14.____
15.____

16. To transmit power economically over considerable distances, it is necessary that the voltage be high. High voltages are *readily* obtainable with _____ current.
    A. d.c.   B. a.c.   C. rectified   D. carrier

16.____

17. With reference to the preceding question, the one *favorable* economic factor in the transmission of power by using high voltages is the
    A. reduction of conductor cross section
    B. decreased amount of insulation required by the line
    C. increased I^2R loss
    D. decreased size of generating stations

17.____

18. The electric meter NOT in itself capable of measuring both d.c. and a.c. voltages is the _____ voltmeter.
    A. D'Arsonval   B. electrodynamometer
    C. iron vane   D. inclined-coil

18.____

3 (#3)

19. The hot wire voltmeter
    A. is a high precision instrument
    B. is used only for d.c. circuits
    C. reads equally well on d.c. and/or a.c. circuits
    D. is used only for a.c. circuits

19.____

Questions 20-22.

DIRECTIONS: Questions 20 through 22 are to be answered on the basis of the diagram below.

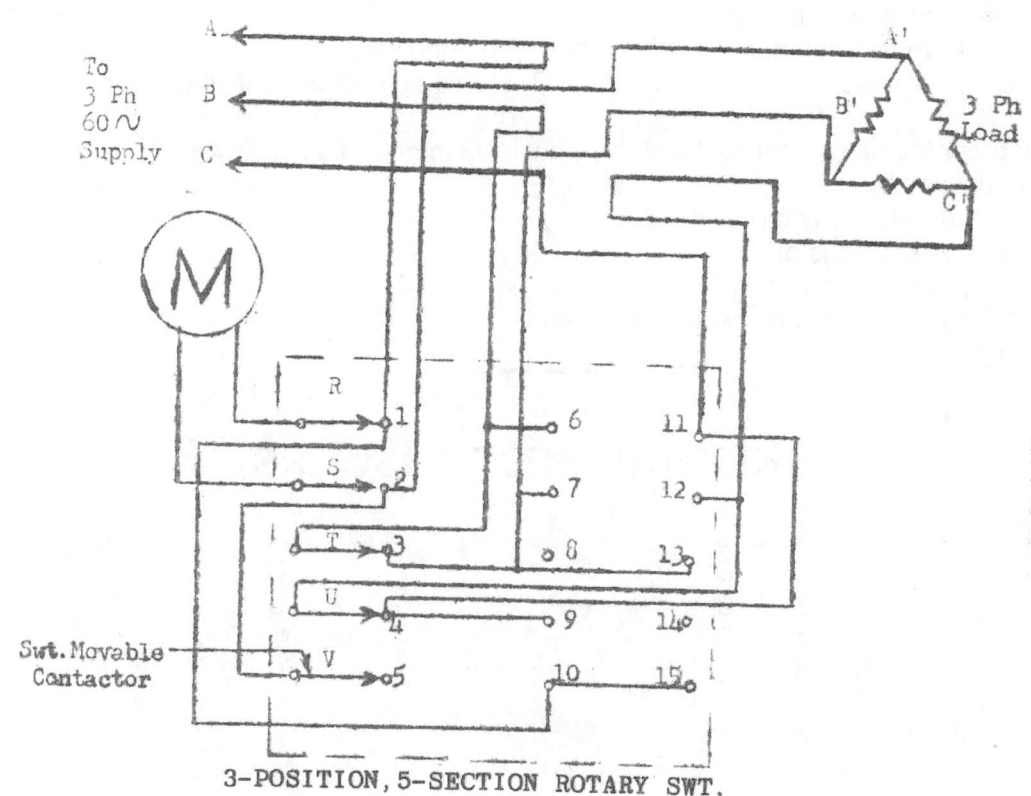

3-POSITION, 5-SECTION ROTARY SWT.

20. With switch movable contacts R, S, T, U and V in position 1, 2, 3, 4, and 5 as shown, Meter M is connected between points _____ and load is _____ connected to supply.
    A. A-A'; improperly
    B. A-A'; properly
    C. C-C'; improperly
    D. C-C'; properly

20.____

21. With switch movable contactors R, S, T, U and V in position 6, 7, 8, 9 and 10, the function of Meter M is to measure the
    A. current in line B-B'
    B. voltage in line B-B'
    C. power drawn by the load
    D. power factor of the load

21.____

51

4 (#3)

22. With switch movable contactors R, S, T, U and V in position 11, 12, 13, 14 and 15, Meter M is connected between points _____ and load is _____ connected to supply.
   A. A-A'; improperly
   B. A-A'; properly
   C. C-C'; improperly
   D. C-C'; properly

22.____

23. To increase the range of d.c. ammeters, you would use a(n)
   A. current transformer
   B. inductance
   C. condenser
   D. shunt

23.____

24. To increase the range of an a.c. ammeter, the one of the following which is MOST commonly used is a(n)
   A. current transformer
   B. inductance
   C. condenser
   D. straight shunt (not U-shaped)

24.____

25. In order to properly connect a single-phase wattmeter to a circuit, you should use two
   A. current and two potential leads
   B. current leads only
   C. potential leads only
   D. current leads and two power leads

25.____

KEY (CORRECT ANSWERS)

1.	C		11.	A
2.	D		12.	N
3.	C		13.	M
4.	B		14.	O
5.	C		15.	P
6.	H		16.	B
7.	E		17.	A
8.	G		18.	A
9.	D		19.	C
10.	F		20.	B

21.	A
22.	D
23.	D
24.	A
25.	A

TEST 4

DIRECTIONS: Each question or incomplete statement is followed by several suggested answers or completions. Select the one that BEST answers the question or completes the statement. *PRINT THE LETTER OF THE CORRECT ANSWER IN THE SPACE AT THE RIGHT.*

Questions 1-2.

DIRECTIONS: Questions 1 and 2 are to be answered on the basis of the following diagram.

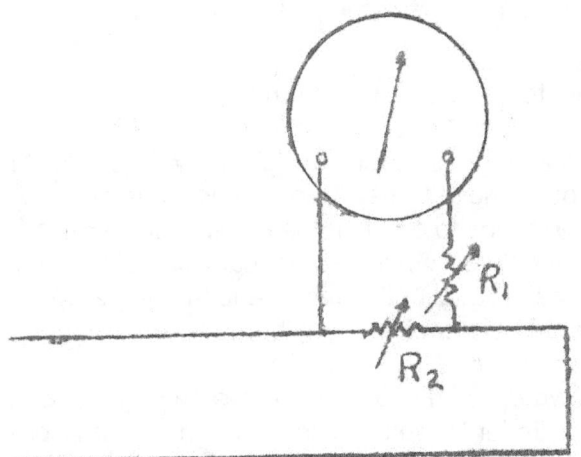

1. The above diagram represents the circuit of a d.c. ammeter. If the value of R_1 is increased while the value of R_2 remains unchanged, the
   A. deflection of the instrument is no longer proportional to the current
   B. range of the ammeter is decreased
   C. range of the ammeter remains the same
   D. range of the ammeter is increased

   1.____

2. In reference to the above diagram, if the value of R_2 is decreased while the value of R_1 remains unchanged, the
   A. range of the ammeter is increased
   B. range of the ammeter is decreased
   C. range of the ammeter remains the same
   D. deflection of the instrument is no longer proportional to the current

   2.____

3. In multiple-conductor armored cable construction, a color scheme is used for identifying purposes. The color-coding of a 3-conductor cable should be which one of the following?
   A. One white, one red, and one black
   B. Two black and one white
   C. Two white and one black
   D. One white, one black, and one blue

   3.____

4. To properly make a short Western Union splice, the competent electrician should understand the common splicing rules. The one of the following which is NOT a common splicing rule is:
   A. Wires of the same size should be spliced together in line.
   B. A joint, or splice, must be as mechanically strong as the wire itself.
   C. A splice must provide a path for the electric current that will be as good as another wire.
   D. All splices must be mechanically and electrically secured by means of solder.

Question 5.

DIRECTIONS: Question 5 refers to the following statement.

The ampere-turns acting on a magnetic circuit are given by the product of the turns lined by the amperes flowing through these turns. Magnetomotive force tends to drive the flux through the circuit and corresponds to e.m.f. in the electric circuit. It is directly proportional to the ampere-turns and only differs from the numerical value of the ampere-turns by the constant factor 1.257, and the product of this factor and the ampere-turns equals the magnetomotive force. This unit of m.m.f. is the gilbert.

5. One pole of a d.c. motor is wound with 500 turns of wire, through which a current of 2 amperes flows. Under these conditions, the m.m.f., in gilberts, acting on this magnetic circuit is *most nearly*
   A. 1,000   B. 1,257   C. 500   D. 628

6. The flux *commonly* used for soldering electrical wire is
   A. tin chloride   B. zinc chloride
   C. rosin   D. silver amalgam

7. The operation of electrical apparatus such as generators, motors, and transformers depends *fundamentally* on induced
   A. permeance   B. e.m.f.   C. reluctance   D. permeability

8. If an inductive circuit carrying current is short-circuited, the current in the circuit will
   A. cease to flow immediately
   B. continue to flow indefinitely
   C. continue to flow for an appreciable time after the instant of short circuit
   D. increase greatly

9. With reference to a.c. supply circuits, the waves of voltage and current *ordinarily* encountered in practice are _____ waves.
   A. sine   B. triangular   C. circular   D. rectangular

Questions 10-12.

DIRECTIONS: Questions 10 through 12 are to be answered on the basis of the following diagram.

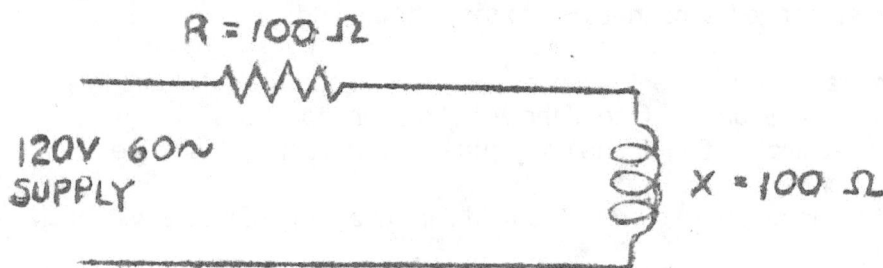

10. The value of the impedance, in ohms, of the above circuit is *most nearly*
    A. 200	B. 50	C. 150	D. 140

11. The current, in amperes, flowing in the above circuit is *most nearly*
    A. .6	B. 2.4	C. 1.2	D. .85

12. The power, in watts, consumed in the above circuit is *most nearly*
    A. 72	B. 144	C. 576	D. 36

13. The power, in watts, taken by a load connected to a three-phase circuit is *generally* expressed by
    A. EI P.F. $\sqrt{2}$	B. EI P.F.	C. $\sqrt{3}$ EI P.F.	D. EI/$\sqrt{3}$ P.F.

14. Three 100-ohm resistances are connected in wye (Y) across a 208-volt, 3-phase circuit. The line current, in amperes, is *approximately*
    A. 6.24	B. 3.6	C. 2.08	D. 1.2

15. An a.c. ammeter is calibrated to read R.M.S. values. This also means that this meter is calibrated to read the _____ value.
    A. average	B. peak	C. effective	D. square

16. An a.c. current of one ampere R.M.S. flowing through a resistance of 10 ohms has the same heating value as a d.c. current of _____ ampere(s) flowing through a _____ resistance.
    A. one; 10-ohm	B. one; 5-ohm	C. two; 10-ohm	D. five; 1-ohm

17. In the common 3-phase, 4-wire supply system, the voltage (in volts) from line to neutral is *most nearly*
    A. 110	B. 120	C. 208	D. 220

18. With reference to the preceding question, the neutral line
    A. does not carry current at any time
    B. carries current at all times
    C. has a potential difference with respect to ground of approximately zero volts
    D. has a potential difference with respect to ground of 208 volts

19. To *reverse* the direction of rotation of a repulsion motor you should
    A. move the brushes so that they cross the pole axis
    B. interchange the connection of either the main or auxiliary winding
    C. interchange the connections to the armature winding
    D. interchange the connections to the field winding

19.____

20. The ordinary direct current series motor does not operate satisfactorily with alternating current. One of the MAIN reasons for this is
    A. excessive heating due to eddy currents in the solid parts of the field structure
    B. that the armature current and field current are out of phase with each other
    C. that the field flux lags 120° in time phase with respect to the line voltage
    D. excessive heating due to the low voltage drop in the series field

20.____

21. If the full rating of a transformer is 90 KV at 90% power factor, then the KVA rating is
    A. 81 B. 90 C. 100 D. 141

21.____

22. A 10-ampere cartridge fuse provided with a navy blue label has a voltage rating, in volts, of
    A. 220 B. 250 C. 550 D. 600

22.____

23. The electrical code states that electrical metallic tubing shall not be used for interior wiring systems of more than 600 volts, nor for conductors *larger than* No.
    A. 6 B. 4 C. 2 D. 0

23.____

24. The diameter of one strand of an electrical conductor having 7 strands is .0305". The size of the conductor, in C.M., is *most nearly*
    A. 13090 B. 10380 C. 6510 D. 4107

24.____

25. To *properly* start a 15 HP d.c. compound motor, you should use a
    A. transformer   B. 4-point starting rheostat
    C. compensator   D. diverter

25.____

KEY (CORRECT ANSWERS)

1. D
2. A
3. A
4. D
5. B

6. C
7. B
8. C
9. A
10. D

11. D
12. A
13. C
14. D
15. C

16. A
17. B
18. C
19. A
20. A

21. C
22. B
23. D
24. C
25. B

TEST 5

DIRECTIONS: Each question or incomplete statement is followed by several suggested answers or completions. Select the one that BEST answers the question or completes the statement. *PRINT THE LETTER OF THE CORRECT ANSWER IN THE SPACE AT THE RIGHT.*

Questions 1-10.

DIRECTIONS: Questions 1 through 10 refer to the material given below. Column I lists definitions of terms used by the electrical code. Column II lists these terms. For each definition listed in Column I, select the term from Column II which it defines and write the letter which precedes the term.

COLUMN I

1. Current consuming equipment fixed or portable

2. That portion of a wiring system extending beyond the final overcurrent device protecting the circuit

3. Any conductors of a wiring system between the main switchboard or point of distribution and the branch circuit overcurrent device

4. Not readily accessible to persons unless special means for access are used

5. A point on the wiring system at which current is taken to supply fixtures, lamps, heaters, motors and current consuming equipment

6. The rigid steel conduit that encloses service entrance conductors

7. That portion of overhead service conductors between the last line pole and the first point of attachment to the building

8. Conductors of a wiring system between the lines of the public utility company or other source of supply and the main switchboard or point of distribution

COLUMN II

A. Mains
B. Switchboard
C. Fuse
D. Outlet
E. Service raceway
F. Feeder
G. Isolated
H. Appliances
J. Branch circuit
K. Fitting
L. Conductor
M. Enclosed
N. Surrounded
O. Service drop

1.____

2.____

3.____

4.____

5.____

6.____

7.____

8.____

9. A wire or cable or other form of metal suitable for carrying electrical energy 9.____

10. Surrounded by a case which will prevent accidental contact with live parts 10.____

Questions 11-12.

DIRECTIONS: Questions 11 and 12 are to be answered on the basis of Figure I below.

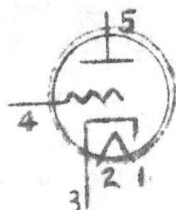

Figure I

11. The above diagram in Figure I is a *commonly* used symbol for a vacuum tube and represents which one of the following types of tubes? 11.____
    A. Triode B. Tetrode C. Pentode D. Heptode

12. Tube element No. 5 is *usually* called the 12.____
    A. grid B. plate C. filament D. cathode

Questions 13-14.

DIRECTIONS: Questions 13 and 14 are to be answered on the basis of Figure II below.

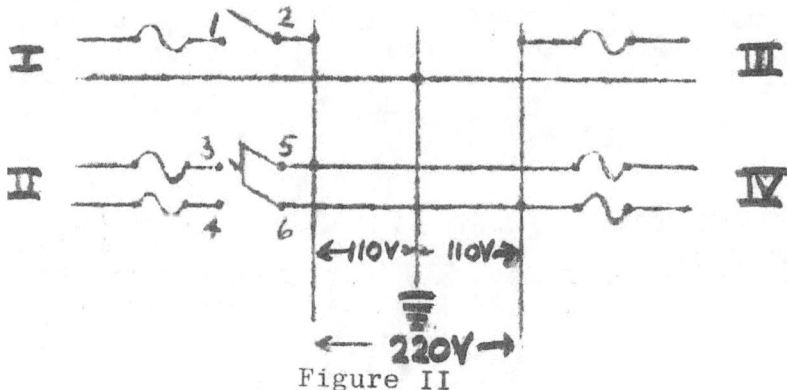

Figure II

13. Circuit No. I in the above diagram 13.____
    A. is not properly fused as it should have one fuse in each leg
    B. supplies 220 volts to the load
    C. is grounded if a pair of test lamps light when placed between point 2 and ground
    D. supplies 110 volts to the load at the board

14. Circuit No. II in the above diagram 14._____
    A. is not properly fused as it should have only one fuse in the hot leg
    B. supplies 110 volts to the load at the board
    C. is grounded if a pair of test lamps light up when placed between points 5 and 6
    D. is grounded if, with the switch in the open position, test lamps light up when placed between points 3 and 5

15. To *properly* start a 15 HP, 3-phase induction motor, you should use a 15._____
    A. shunt   B. 4-point starting rheostat
    C. compensator   D. diverter

Questions 16-25.

DIRECTIONS: Questions 16 through 25 refer to the material given below. Column I lists items which are represented by symbols listed in Column II. For each item in Column I, select the appropriate symbol from Column II which it represents and write the letter which precedes the symbol.

COLUMN I   COLUMN II

16. Lighting panel   A. [symbol]   16._____

17. Special purpose outlet   B. [symbol]   17._____

18. Floor outlet   C. S_3 18._____

19. Three-way switch   D. [symbol]   19._____

20. Normally closed contact   E. [symbol]   20._____

21. Resistor   F. [symbol]   21._____

22. Watt-hour meter   G. [symbol]   22._____

23. Two-pole electrically operated   H. [symbol]   23._____
    contactor with blowout coil
                                          J. [symbol]
24. Capacitor   24._____
                                          K. [symbol]
25. Bell   25._____
                                          L. [symbol]

                                          M. [symbol]

KEY (CORRECT ANSWERS)

1. H
2. J
3. F
4. G
5. D

6. E
7. O
8. A
9. L
10. M

11. A
12. B
13. D
14. D
15. C

16. B
17. D
18. E
19. C
20. F

21. G
22. K
23. J
24. H
25. A

TEST 6

DIRECTIONS: Each question or incomplete statement is followed by several suggested answers or completions. Select the one that BEST answers the question or completes the statement. *PRINT THE LETTER OF THE CORRECT ANSWER IN THE SPACE AT THE RIGHT.*

Questions 1-8.

DIRECTIONS: Questions 1 through 8 are to be answered on the basis of the figures below. Each question gives the proper figure to use with that question.

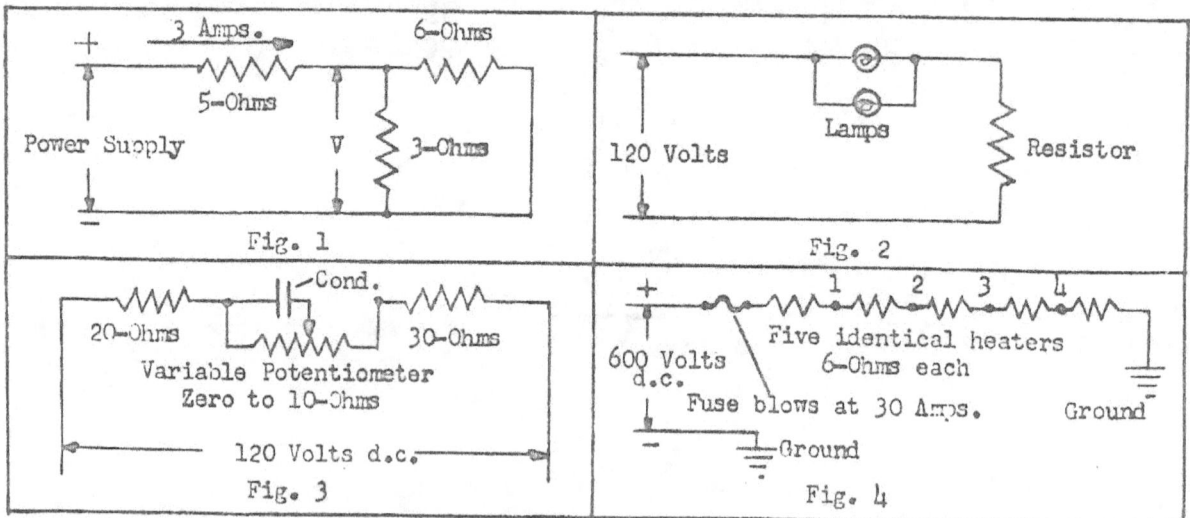

1. In Figure 1, the voltage V is _____ volts.
   A. 27   B. 9   C. 6   D. 3

2. In Figure 1, the current in the 6-ohm resistor is _____ ampere(s).
   A. 3   B. 2   C. 1.6   D. 1

3. In Figure 2, each lamp is to take 1 ampere at 20 volts. The resistor should be _____ ohms.
   A. 100   B. 80   C. 50   D. 40

4. In Figure 3, the MAXIMUM voltage which can be placed across the condenser by varying the potentiometer is _____ volts.
   A. 120   B. 60   C. 40   D. 20

5. In Figure 3, the MINIMUM voltage which can be placed across the condenser by varying the potentiometer is _____ volts.
   A. 60   B. 40   C. 20   D. zero

6. In Figure 4, the heater circuit is normally completed through the two ground connections shown. If an accidental ground occurs at point 4, then the number of heaters which will heat up is
   A. five   B. four   C. one   D. none

7. In Figure 4, the fuse will NOT blow with a ground at point
   A. 1   B. 2   C. 3   D. 4

8. In Figure 4, if a short occurs from point 2 to point 3, then the number of heaters which will heat up is
   A. five   B. four   C. two   D. none

Questions 9-16.

DIRECTIONS: Questions 9 through 16 are to be answered on the basis of the wiring diagram below. Refer to this diagram when answering these questions.

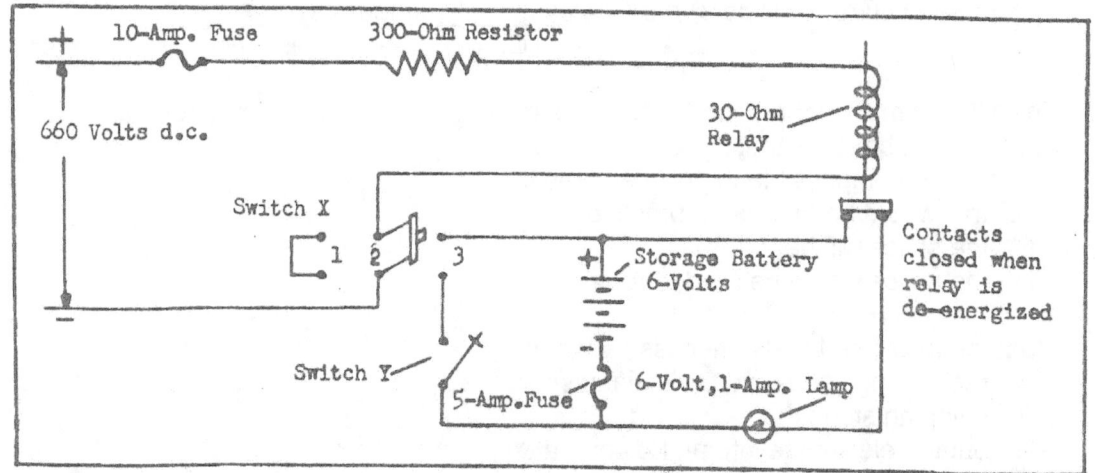

9. Throwing switch X to Position No. 1 will
   A. charge the battery
   B. energize the lamp
   C. energize the relay
   D. blow the 5-ampere fuse

10. With switch X in Position No. 1, the 10-ampere fuse will blow if a dead short occurs across the
    A. 300-ohm resistor
    B. relay coil
    C. battery
    D. lamp

11. With switch X in Position No. 2, the current through the 300-ohm resistor will be
    A. zero   B. 2 amperes   C. 2.2 amperes   D. 10 amperes

12. With switch X in Position No. 3 and switch Y open, the current taken from the battery will be
    A. zero B. 1 ampere C. 5 amperes D. 10 amperes

13. With switch Y in the open position and the relay contacts open, the
    A. lamp will be lit
    B. lamp will be dark
    C. battery will be discharging
    D. 5-ampere fuse will be overloaded

14. The battery will charge with switch X in Position No. _____ and switch Y _____.
    A. 3; closed B. 3; open C. 1; closed D. 1; open

15. With the relay contacts closed, a dead short across the lamp will
    A. blow the 10-ampere fuse
    B. blow the 5-ampere fuse
    C. not blow any fuses
    D. cause the battery to charge

16. When the switches are set to the positions which will charge the battery, the charging current will be *approximately* _____ ampere(s).
    A. ½ B. 2 C. 5 D. 10

17. The MOST important reason for NOT having a power line splice in a conduit run between boxes is that
    A. it will be impossible to pull the wires through
    B. this would be an unsafe practice
    C. the splice will heat up
    D. the splice would be hard to repair

18. Goggles would be LEAST necessary when
    A. recharging soda-acid fire extinguishers
    B. chipping stones
    C. putting electrolyte into an Edison battery
    D. scraping rubber insulation from a wire

19. A commutator and brushes will be found on a(n)
    A. alternator
    B. rotary converter
    C. squirrel-cage induction motor
    D. wound-rotor induction motor

20. In a house bell circuit, the pushbutton for ringing the bell is generally connected in the secondary of the transformer feeding the bell. One reason for this is to
    A. save power
    B. keep line voltage out of the pushbutton circuit
    C. prevent the bell from burning out
    D. prevent arcing of the vibrator contact points in the bell

KEY (CORRECT ANSWERS)

1.	C	11.	A
2.	D	12.	B
3.	C	13.	B
4.	D	14.	A
5.	D	15.	B
6.	B	16.	B
7.	D	17.	B
8.	B	18.	D
9.	C	19.	B
10.	A	20.	B

EXAMINATION SECTION
TEST 1

DIRECTIONS: Each question or incomplete statement is followed by several suggested answers or completions. Select the one that BEST answers the question or completes the statement. *PRINT THE LETTER OF THE CORRECT ANSWER IN THE SPACE AT THE RIGHT.*

Questions 1-6.

DIRECTIONS: Questions 1 through 6 are to be answered on the basis of the circuit diagram below. All switches are initially open.

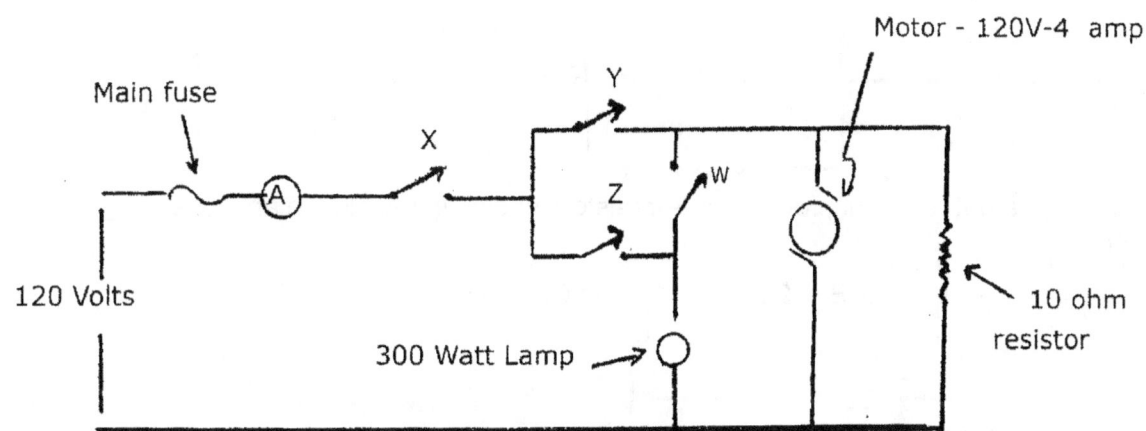

1. To light the 300 watt lamp, the following switches MUST be closed: 1.____

   A. X and Y   B. Y and Z   C. X and Z   D. X and W

2. If all of the switches W, X, Y, and Z are closed, the following will happen: 2.____

   A. The lamp will light and the motor will rotate
   B. The lamp will light and the motor will not rotate
   C. The lamp will not light and the motor will not rotate
   D. A short circuit will occur and the main fuse will blow

3. With 120 volts applied across the 10 ohm resistor, the current drawn by the resistor is _____ amp(s).   3.____

   A. 1/12   B. 1.2   C. 12   D. 1200

4. With 120 volts applied to the 10 ohm resistor, the power used by the resistor is _____ kw.   4.____

   A. 1.44   B. 1.2   C. .144   D. .12

5. The current drawn by the 300 watt lamp when lighted should be APPROXIMATELY _____ amps.   5.____

   A. 2.5   B. 3.6   C. 25   D. 36

67

6. In the circuit shown, the symbol A is used to indicate a (n)
   A. ammeter
   B. *and* circuit
   C. voltmeter
   D. wattmeter

7. Of the following materials, the BEST conductor of electricity is
   A. iron
   B. copper
   C. aluminum
   D. glass

8. The sum of 6'6", 5'9", and 2' 1 1/2" is
   A. 13'4 1/2"
   B. 13'6 1/2"
   C. 14'4 1/2"
   D. 14'6 1/2"

9.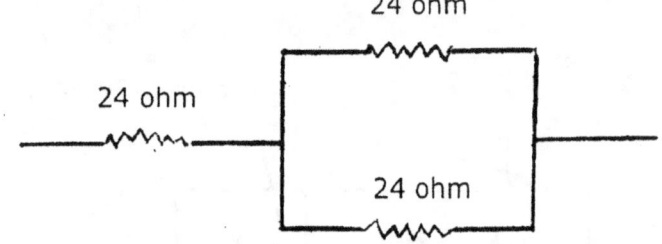

   The equivalent resistance of the three resistors shown in the sketch above is _____ ohms.
   A. 8
   B. 24
   C. 36
   D. 72

10.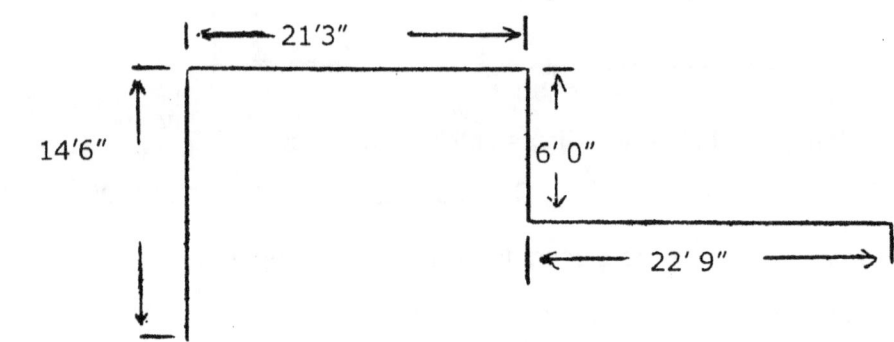

    The TOTAL length of electrical conduit that must be run along the path shown on the diagram above is
    A. 63'8"
    B. 64'6"
    C. 65'6"
    D. 66'8"

11. Of the following electrical devices, the one that is NOT normally used in direct current electrical circuits is a (n)
    A. circuit breaker
    B. double-pole switch
    C. transformer
    D. inverter

12. The number of 120-volt light bulbs that should NORMALLY be connected in series across a 600-volt electric line is
    A. 1
    B. 2
    C. 3
    D. 5

13. Of the following motors, the one that does NOT have any brushes is the _____ motor.

    A. d.c. shunt
    B. d.c. series
    C. squirrel cage induction
    D. compound

14. Of the following materials, the one that is COMMONLY used as an electric heating element in an electric heater is

    A. zinc
    B. brass
    C. terne plate
    D. nichrome

Questions 15-25.

DIRECTIONS: Questions 15 through 25 are to be answered on the basis of the instruments listed below. Each instrument is listed with an identifying number in front of it.

    1 - Hygrometer
    2 - Ammeter
    3 - Voltmeter
    4 - Wattmeter
    5 - Megger
    6 - Oscilloscope
    7 - Frequency meter
    8 - Micrometer
    9 - Vernier caliper
    10 - Wire gage
    11 - 6-foot folding rule
    12 - Architect's scale
    13 - Planimeter
    14 - Engineer's scale
    15 - Ohmmeter

15. The instrument that should be used to accurately measure the resistance of a 4,700 ohm resistor is Number

    A. 3   B. 4   C. 7   D. 15

16. To measure the current in an electrical circuit, the instrument that should be used is Number

    A. 2   B. 7   C. 8   D. 15

17. To measure the insulation resistance of a rubber-covered electrical cable, the instrument that should be used is Number

    A. 4   B. 5   C. 8   D. 15

18. An AC motor is hooked up to a power distribution box.
    In order to check the voltage at the motor terminals, the instrument that should be used is Number

    A. 2   B. 3   C. 4   D. 7

19. To measure the shaft diameter of a motor accurately to one-thousandth of an inch, the instrument that should be used is Number

    A. 8   B. 10   C. 11   D. 14

20. The instrument that should be used to determine whether 25 Hz. or 60 Hz. is present in an electrical circuit is Number

    A. 4   B. 5   C. 7   D. 8

21. Of the following, the PROPER instrument to use to determine the diameter of the conductor of a piece of electrical hook-up wire is Number

    A. 10   B. 11   C. 12   D. 14

22. The amount of electrical power being used in a balanced three-phase circuit should be measured with Number

    A. 2   B. 3   C. 4   D. 5

23. The electrical wave form at a given point in an electronic circuit can be observed with Number

    A. 2   B. 3   C. 6   D. 7

24. The PROPER instrument to use for measuring the width of a door is Number

    A. 11   B. 12   C. 13   D. 14

25. A one-inch hole with a tolerance of plus or minus three-thousandths is reamed in a steel block.
    The PROPER instrument to use to accurately check the diameter of the hole is Number

    A. 8   B. 9   C. 11   D. 14

KEY (CORRECT ANSWERS)

1. C	11. C
2. A	12. D
3. C	13. C
4. A	14. D
5. A	15. D
6. A	16. A
7. B	17. B
8. C	18. B
9. C	19. A
10. B	20. C

21. A
22. C
23. C
24. A
25. B

TEST 2

DIRECTIONS: Each question or incomplete statement is followed by several suggested answers or completions. Select the one that BEST answers the question or completes the statement. *PRINT THE LETTER OF THE CORRECT ANSWER IN THE SPACE AT THE RIGHT.*

1. The number of conductors required to connect a 3-phase delta connected heater bank to an electric power panel board is

    A. 2   B. 3   C. 4   D. 5

2. Of the following, the wire size that is MOST commonly used for branch lighting circuits in homes is _____ A.W.G.

    A. #12   B. #8   C. #6   D. #4

3. When installing electrical circuits, the tool that should be used to pull wire through a conduit is a

    A. mandrel
    B. snake
    C. rod
    D. pulling iron

4. Of the following AC voltages, the LOWEST voltage that a neon test lamp can detect is _____ volts.

    A. 6   B. 12   C. 80   D. 120

5. Of the following, the BEST procedure to use when storing tools that are subject to rusting is to

    A. apply a thin coating of soap onto the tools
    B. apply a light coating of oil to the tools
    C. wrap the tools in clean cheesecloth
    D. place the tools in a covered container

6. If a 3 1/2 inch long nail is required to nail wood framing members together, the nail size to use should be

    A. 2d   B. 4d   C. 16d   D. 60d

7. Of the four motors listed below, the one that can operate only on alternating current is a(n) _____ motor.

    A. series
    B. shunt
    C. compound
    D. induction

8. The sum of 1/3 + 2/5 + 5/6 is

    A. 1 17/30   B. 1 3/5   C. 1 15/24   D. 1 5/6

9. Of the following instruments, the one that should be used to measure the state of charge of a lead-acid storage battery is a(n)

    A. ammeter
    B. ohmmeter
    C. hydrometer
    D. thermometer

71

10. If three 1 1/2 volt dry cell batteries are wired in series, the TOTAL voltage provided by the three batteries is _____ volts.

   A. 1.5   B. 3   C. 4.5   D. 6.0

11. Taking into account time and one-half payment for time over 40 hours of work, the gross pay of an employee who works 43 hours in a week at a rate of pay of $10.68 per hour is

   A. $427.20   B. $459.24   C. $475.26   D. $491.28

12. The sum of 0.365 + 3.941 + 10.676 + 0.784 is

   A. 13.766   B. 15.666   C. 15.756   D. 15.766

13. In order to transmit mechanical power between two rotating shafts at right angles to each other, two gears are used. Of the following, the type of gears that should be used are _____ gears.

   A. herringbone   B. spur
   C. bevel   D. rack and pinion

14. To properly ground the service electrical equipment in a building, a ground connection should be made to _____ the building.

   A. the waste or soil line leaving
   B. the vent line going to the exterior of
   C. any steel beam in
   D. the cold water line entering

15. The area of the triangle shown at the right is _____ square inches.
   A. 120
   B. 240
   C. 360
   D. 480

Questions 16-25.

DIRECTIONS: Questions 16 through 25 are to be answered on the basis of the tools shown on the next page. The tools are not shown to scale. Each tool is shown with an identifying number alongside it.

3 (#2)

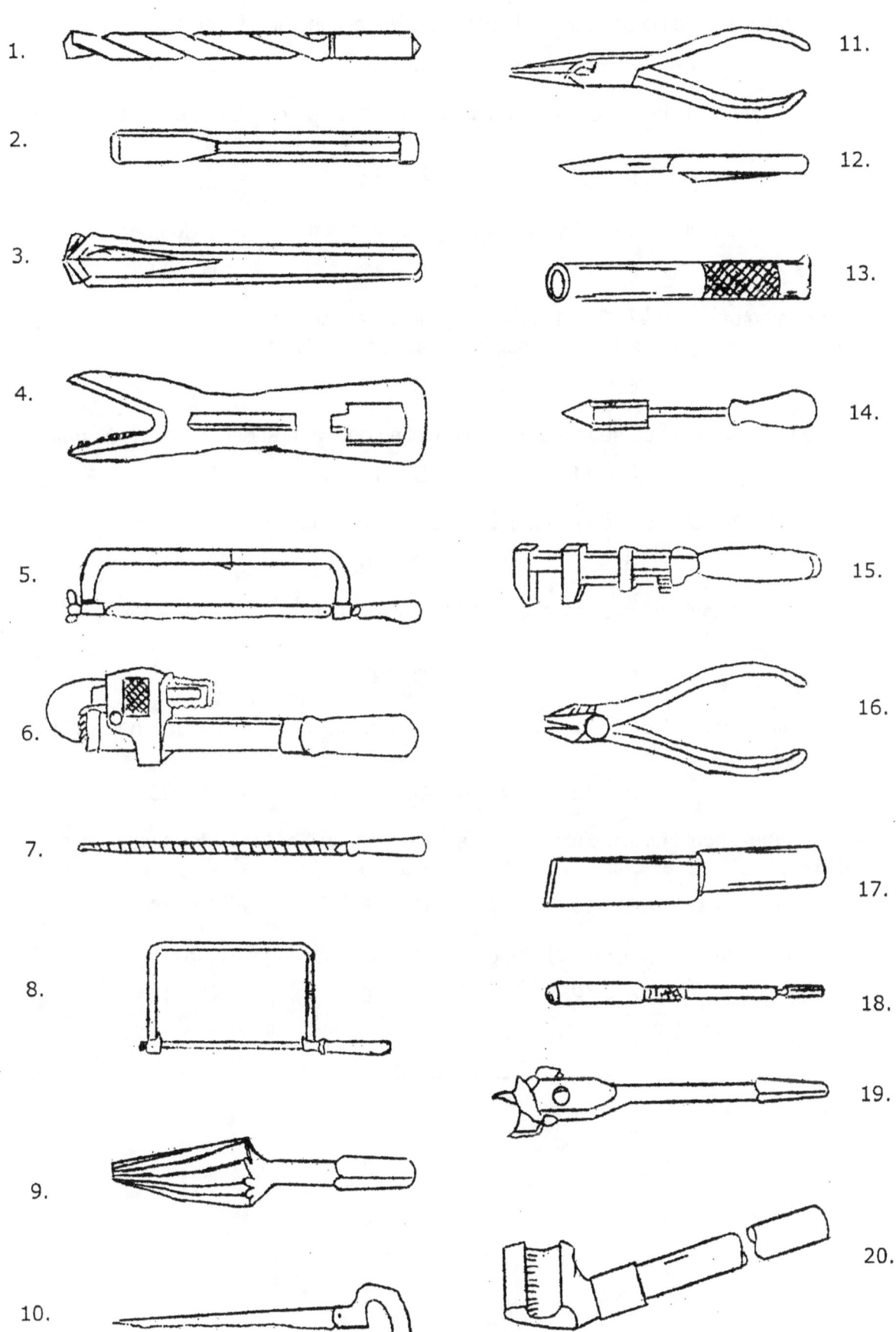

73

16. The tool that should be used for cutting thin wall steel conduit is Number

    A. 5   B. 8   C. 10   D. 16

17. The tool that should be used for cutting a 1 7/8 inch diameter hole in a wood joist is Number

    A. 3   B. 9   C. 14   D. 19

18. The tool that should be used for soldering splices in electrical wire is Number

    A. 3   B. 7   C. 13   D. 14

19. After cutting off a piece of 3/4 inch diameter electrical conduit, the tool that should be used for removing a burr from the inside of the conduit is Number

    A. 9   B. 11   C. 12   D. 14

20. The tool that should be used for turning a coupling onto a threaded conduit is Number

    A. 6   B. 11   C. 15   D. 16

21. The tool that should be used for cutting wood lathing in plaster walls is Number

    A. 5   B. 7   C. 10   D. 12

22. The tool that should be used for drilling a 3/8 inch diameter hole in a steel beam is Number

    A. 1   B. 2   C. 3   D. 9

23. Of the following, the BEST tool to use for stripping insulation from electrical hook-up wire is Number

    A. 11   B. 12   C. 15   D. 20

24. The tool that should be used for bending an electrical wire around a terminal post is Number

    A. 4   B. 11   C. 15   D. 16

25. The tool that should be used for cutting electrical hookup wire is Number

    A. 5   B. 12   C. 16   D. 17

KEY (CORRECT ANSWERS)

1.	B	11.	C
2.	A	12.	D
3.	B	13.	C
4.	C	14.	D
5.	B	15.	A
6.	C	16.	A
7.	D	17.	D
8.	A	18.	D
9.	C	19.	A
10.	C	20.	A

21. C
22. A
23. B
24. B
25. C

TEST 3

DIRECTIONS: Each question or incomplete statement is followed by several suggested answers or completions. Select the one that BEST answers the question or completes the statement. *PRINT THE LETTER OF THE CORRECT ANSWER IN THE SPACE AT THE RIGHT.*

1. An electric circuit has current flowing through it. The panel board switch feeding the circuit is opened, causing arcing across the switch contacts.
Generally, this arcing is caused by

   A. a lack of energy storage in the circuit
   B. electrical energy stored by a capacitor
   C. electrical energy stored by a resistor
   D. magnetic energy induced by an inductance

   1.____

2. MOST filter capacitors in radios have a capacity rating given in

   A. microvolts
   C. millihenries
   B. milliamps
   D. microfarads

   2.____

3. Of the following, the electrical wire size that is COMMONLY used for telephone circuits is _____ A.W.G.

   A. #6
   B. #10
   C. #12
   D. #22

   3.____

Questions 4-9.

DIRECTIONS: Questions 4 through 9 are to be answered on the basis of the electrical circuit diagram shown below, where letters are used to identify various circuit components.

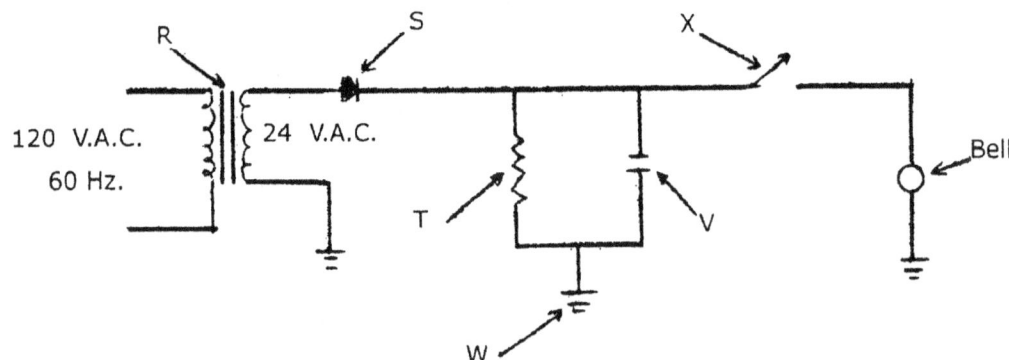

4. The device indicated by the letter R is a

   A. capacitor
   C. resistor
   B. converter
   D. transformer

   4.____

5. The device indicated by the letter S is a

   A. transistor
   C. thermistor
   B. diode
   D. directional relay

   5.____

76

6. The devices indicated by the letters T and V are used together to _____ components of the secondary current.

    A. reduce the AC
    B. reduce the DC
    C. transform the AC
    D. invert the AC

7. The letter W points to a standard electrical symbol for a

    A. wire
    B. ground
    C. terminal
    D. lightning arrestor

8. Closing switch X will apply the following type of voltage to the bell:

    A. 60 Hz. AC
    B. DC
    C. pulsating AC
    D. 120 Hz. AC

9. The circuit shown contains a _____ rectifier.

    A. mercury-arc
    B. full-wave
    C. bridge
    D. half-wave

10. A bolt specified as 1/4-28 means the following:
    The

    A. bolt is 1/4 inch in diameter and has 28 threads per inch
    B. bolt is 1/4 inch in diameter and is 2.8 inches long
    C. bolt is 1/4 inch long and has 28 threads
    D. threaded portion of the bolt is 1/4 inch long and has 28 threads per inch

11. When cutting 0.045-inch thickness sheet metal, it is BEST to use a hacksaw blade that has _____ teeth per inch.

    A. 7
    B. 12
    C. 18
    D. 32

12. To accurately tighten a bolt to 28 foot-pounds, it is BEST to use a(n) _____ wrench.

    A. pipe
    B. open end
    C. box
    D. torque

13. When bending a 2-inch diameter conduit, the CORRECT tool to use is a

    A. hickey
    B. pipe wrench
    C. hydraulic bender
    D. stock and die

14. When soldering two #20 A.W.G. copper wires together to form a splice, the solder that SHOULD be used is _____ solder.

    A. acid-core
    B. solid-core
    C. rosin-core
    D. liquid

15. A bathroom heating unit draws 10 amperes at 115 volts.
    The hot resistance of the heating unit should be _____ ohms.

    A. .08
    B. 8
    C. 11.5
    D. 1150

16. Of the following materials, the one that is NOT suitable as an electrical insulator is

    A. glass
    B. mica
    C. rubber
    D. platinum

17. An air conditioning unit is rated at 1000 watts. The unit is run for 10 hours per day, five days per week.
If the cost for electrical energy is 5 cents per kilowatt-hour, the weekly cost for electricity should be

    A. 25¢ B. 50¢ C. $2.50 D. $25.00

17._____

18. If a fuse is protecting the circuit of a 15 ohm electric heater and it is designed to blow out at a current exceeding 10 amperes, the MAXIMUM voltage from among the following that should be applied across the terminals of the heater is _____ volts.

    A. 110 B. 120 C. 160 D. 600

18._____

19. Before opening a pneumatic hose connection, it is important to remove pressure from the hose line PRIMARILY to avoid

    A. losing air
    B. personal injury
    C. damage to the hose connection
    D. a build-up of pressure in the air compressor

19._____

20. If the scale on a shop drawing is 1/4 inch to the foot, then a part which measures 3 3/8 inches long on the drawing has an ACTUAL length of _____ feet _____ inches.

    A. 12; 6 B. 13; 6 C. 13; 9 D. 14; 9

20._____

21. The function that is USUALLY performed by a motor controller is to

    A. start and stop a motor
    B. protect a motor from a short circuit
    C. prevent bearing failure of a motor
    D. control the brush wear in a motor

21._____

22. Of the following galvanized sheet metal electrical outlet boxes, the one that is NOT a commonly used size is the _____ box.

    A. 4" square
    C. 4" x 2 1/8"
    B. 4" octagonal
    D. 4" x 1"

22._____

23. When soldering a transistor into a circuit, it is MOST important to protect the transistor from

    A. the application of an excess of rosin flux
    B. excessive heat
    C. the application of an excess of solder
    D. too much pressure

23._____

24. When installing BX type cable, it is important to protect the wires in the cable from the cut ends of the armored sheath.
The APPROVED method of providing this protection is to

    A. use a fiber or plastic insulating bushing
    B. file the cut ends of the sheath smooth
    C. use a connector where the cable enters a junction box
    D. tie the wires into an Underwriter's knot

24._____

25. While lifting a heavy piece of equipment off the floor, a person should NOT

   A. twist his body
   B. grasp it firmly
   C. maintain a solid footing on the ground
   D. bend his knees

26. It is important that metal cabinets and panels that house electrical equipment should be grounded PRIMARILY in order to

   A. prevent short circuits from occurring
   B. keep all circuits at ground potential
   C. minimize shock hazards
   D. reduce the effects of electrolytic corrosion

27. A foreman explains a technical procedure to a new employee. If the employee does not understand the instructions he has received, it would be BEST if he were to

   A. follow the procedure as best he could
   B. ask the foreman to explain it to him again
   C. avoid following the procedure
   D. ask the foreman to give him other work

28. Of the following, the BEST connectors to use when mounting an electrical panel box directly onto a concrete wall are

   A. threaded studs   B. machine screws
   C. lag screws   D. expansion bolts

29. Of the following, the BEST instrument to use to measure the small gap between relay contacts is

   A. a micrometer   B. a feeler gage
   C. inside calipers   D. a plug gage

30. A POSSIBLE result of mounting a 40 ampere fuse in a fuse box for a circuit requiring a 20 ampere fuse is that the 40 ampere fuse may

   A. provide twice as much protection to the circuit from overloads
   B. blow more easily than the smaller fuse due to an overload
   C. cause serious damage to the circuit from an overload
   D. reduce power consumption in the circuit

KEY (CORRECT ANSWERS)

1. D
2. D
3. D
4. D
5. B

6. A
7. B
8. B
9. D
10. A

11. D
12. D
13. C
14. C
15. C

16. D
17. C
18. B
19. B
20. B

21. A
22. D
23. B
24. A
25. A

26. C
27. B
28. D
29. B
30. C

EXAMINATION SECTION
TEST 1

DIRECTIONS: Each question or incomplete statement is followed by several suggested answers or completions. Select the one that BEST answers the question or completes the statement. *PRINT THE LETTER OF THE CORRECT ANSWER IN THE SPACE AT THE RIGHT.*

1. A piece of equipment listed as drawing 100 watts is plugged into a 24 volt DC circuit. The MINIMUM size fuse which would handle this load is _____ amps.

   A. 2   B. 3   C. 4   D. 5

2. A resistor of 1000 ohms has 3 milliamperes passing through it. The voltage drop across the resistor is _____ volts.

   A. 3   B. 6   C. 15   D. 300

3. A certain resistor has three colored bands around it. The one nearest the end is green, the next one is orange, and the next one is red.
   The value of this register is _____ ohms.

   A. 74   B. 270   C. 5300   D. 64,000

4. An alternating voltage is applied to a capacitor.
   As the frequency of this voltage is increased, the impedance of the capacitor

   A. increases
   B. decreases
   C. remains the same
   D. increases or decreases depending on its construction

5. The one of the following that is NOT a part of a transistor is the

   A. emitter   B. collector   C. base   D. grid

6. A 0.2 ufd capacitor is connected in series with a 0.1 ufd capacitor.
   The resultant capacity is _____ ufd.

   A. 0.067   B. 0.67   C. 0.15   D. 0.3

7. The term *Hertz* means the same as

   A. degrees Centigrade   B. degrees Fahrenheit
   C. revolutions per minute   D. cycles per second

8. In an electrolytic condenser, the dielectric material is

   A. mylar   B. aluminum oxide
   C. paper   D. sodium chloride

9. The amount by which a transformer will step up or step down a voltage is determined by its

   A. inductance   B. resistance
   C. magnetic flux   D. turns ratio

10. The electrolyte in a lead plate storage battery (such as that used in cars) is

    A. aluminum hydroxide
    B. sulfuric acid
    C. hydrochloric acid
    D. sodium chloride

11. A diode in an electronic circuit is used to

    A. amplify   B. oscillate   C. attenuate   D. rectify

12. The MAIN function of a filter in a power supply is to

    A. increase the voltage
    B. decrease the load
    C. smooth out the peaks of the ripple frequency
    D. protect the power transformer

13. The expression *pH* as applied to a liquid refers to its

    A. salinity
    B. specific gravity
    C. viscosity
    D. acidity/alkalinity

14. The speed of a synchronous motor is controlled by

    A. the voltage applied to it
    B. the frequency of the alternating current applied to it
    C. a mechanical governor
    D. the current it draws

15. The capacitance of a condenser is measured in

    A. oersteds   B. ohms   C. henrys   D. farads

16. The power lost in a 20-ohm resistor, with 0.25 amperes passing through it, is _____ watts.

    A. 0.04   B. 0.4   C. 1.25   D. 5

17. When soldering a transistor into a circuit, it is good practice to clamp a pair of long-nosed pliers on the lead between the transistor and the end being soldered. This is done to

    A. prevent the lead from moving
    B. prevent burning the fingers
    C. ground the transistor
    D. prevent the soldering iron's heat from reaching the transistor

18. The commutator of a motor should

    A. not be lubricated
    B. be lubricated with light oil
    C. be lubricated with heavy grease
    D. be lubricated with hypoid oil

19. The band of wavelengths of visible light covers

    A. 20-50 centimeters
    B. 10-50 meters
    C. 400-700 millimicrons
    D. 400-700 millimeters

20. The heat reaching the earth from the sun is transmitted by

   A. ions
   B. convection
   C. radiation
   D. cosmic rays

21. A *thermistor* is a

   A. type of thermometer
   B. high power transistor
   C. water heating device
   D. resistor with a negative temperature coefficient

22. In an AC circuit, the term *power factor* refers to the

   A. horsepower
   B. BTU per watt
   C. ratio of the resistance to the impedance
   D. kilowatts per horsepower

23.

   In the above circuit, the TOTAL resistance between points A and B is _____ ohms.

   A. 5   B. 14   C. 20   D. 45

24. Of the four gases listed below, the one that is NOT an air pollutant is

   A. carbon dioxide
   B. carbon monoxide
   C. sulfur dioxide
   D. hydrogen sulfide

25. The term *milli-roentgen* refers to a unit of

   A. x-ray radiation
   B. ultraviolet radiation
   C. reluctance
   D. inductance

26. An AC motor drawing 12 amps is plugged into a 15-amp circuit. The starting surge of the motor, however, is 18 amps.
    The PROPER type of fuse to be used in this situation is

   A. varistor
   B. thermistor
   C. fast-blow
   D. slow-blow

27. Degrees Kelvin is numerically equal to degrees

   A. Fahrenheit - 15
   B. Centigrade + 27
   C. Fahrenheit + 135
   D. Centigrade + 273

28. In the term *micromicrofarads*, the prefix *micromicro* means multiply by

   A. 10^6 B. 10^3 C. 10^{-12} D. 10^{-6}

29. One horsepower is equivalent to

   A. 276 joules
   B. 746 kilowatts
   C. 746 watts
   D. 291 calories

30. Laminated iron or steel is generally used instead of solid metal in the construction of the field and armature cores in motors and generators.
   The reason for this is to

   A. reduce eddy current losses
   B. increase the voltage
   C. decrease the flux
   D. reduce the cost

31. The instrument used to measure current flow is called a(n)

   A. wattmeter
   B. voltmeter
   C. ammeter
   D. wavemeter

32. Reversing the polarity of the voltage applied to a mica condenser will

   A. destroy it
   B. increase its capacity
   C. decrease its capacity
   D. have no effect on it

33. The *decibel* is the unit used for expressing

   A. light levels
   B. DC voltage
   C. AC current
   D. the ratio between two quantities of either electrical or sound energy

34. In a three-phase Y-connected AC power system, the voltage from leg to ground is 120 volts.
   The voltage between each pair of hot legs is _____ volts.

   A. 160   B. 180   C. 208   D. 240

35. An hygrometer is an instrument which measures

   A. humidity
   B. temperature
   C. specific gravity
   D. luminosity

36. The impedance ratio of a transformer varies _____ the turns ratio.

   A. directly with
   B. as the square of
   C. as the square root of
   D. inversely with

37. Two resistors are connected in series. The current through these resistors is 3 amperes. Resistance #1 has a value of fifty ohms; resistance #2 has a voltage drop of fifty volts across its terminals.
   The TOTAL impressed voltage (across both resistors) is _____ volts.

   A. 100   B. 150   C. 200   D. 250

38. The piece of equipment that should be used to obtain more than one voltage from a fixed voltage direct current source is a(n)

   A. multitap transformer
   B. resistance-type voltage divider
   C. autotransformer
   D. copper oxide rectifier

39. The ratio of peak to effective (rms) voltage value of a sine wave is

   A. 2 to 1   B. 1 to 2   C. .707 to 1   D. 1.414 to 1

40. Two coils are connected in series.
    If there is no mutual inductance between the coils, the TOTAL inductance of the two coils is the _____ inductances.

   A. sum of the individual
   B. product of the individual
   C. product of the square roots of the two
   D. sum of the squares of the individual

41. The impedance of a coil with zero resistance is called the

   A. reluctance   B. conductance
   C. inductive reactance   D. flux

42. The ratio of the energy stored to the energy lost in a coil over a period of one cycle is called its

   A. efficiency   B. Q
   C. reactance   D. resistance

43. In a vacuum tube, the current is carried by

   A. ions   B. neutrons   C. electrons   D. molecules

44. The device used to vary the intensity of an incandescent light on a 120V AC circuit is a

   A. variable capacitor
   B. silicon controlled rectifier
   C. copper oxide rectifier
   D. rf amplifier

45. High power transistors must be mounted on *heat sinks*. The purpose of the heat sinks is to

   A. improve voltage regulation
   B. increase the transistors' output
   C. keep the transistors warm
   D. keep the transistors cool

46. The one of the following materials that has the HIGHEST conductivity is

   A. iron   B. zinc   C. copper   D. silver

47. The unit used to express the alternating current impedance of a circuit is the   47.____

    A. mho   B. farad   C. ohm   D. rel

48. A certain resistor has four colored bands on it. The fourth band is gold.   48.____
    This means that the resistor

    A. is wirewound   B. is non-inductive
    C. has a ± 20% tolerance   D. has a ± 5% tolerance

49. An amplifier has an output voltage waveform that does not exactly follow that of the input   49.____
    voltage.
    This type of distortion is called _____ distortion.

    A. modular   B. frequency
    C. resonance   D. amplitude

50. A parallel circuit, resonant at 1000 khz, has its value of capacity doubled and its value of   50.____
    inductance halved.
    Its resonant frequency now is _____ khz.

    A. 500   B. 1000   C. 1500   D. 2000

KEY (CORRECT ANSWERS)

1. D	11. D	21. D	31. C	41. C
2. A	12. C	22. C	32. D	42. B
3. C	13. D	23. B	33. D	43. C
4. B	14. B	24. A	34. C	44. B
5. D	15. D	25. A	35. A	45. D
6. A	16. C	26. D	36. B	46. D
7. D	17. D	27. D	37. C	47. C
8. B	18. A	28. C	38. B	48. D
9. D	19. C	29. C	39. D	49. D
10. B	20. C	30. A	40. A	50. B

TEST 2

DIRECTIONS: Each question or incomplete statement is followed by several suggested answers or completions. Select the one that BEST answers the question or completes the statement. *PRINT THE LETTER OF THE CORRECT ANSWER IN THE SPACE AT THE RIGHT.*

1. A voltmeter which reads 100V full scale has a specified accuracy of 3%. It is hooked across a circuit and reads 97 volts.
   The TRUE voltage can be assumed to be somewhere between

   A. 96.7 and 97.3 B. 94 and 100
   C. 96.07 and 97.03 D. 95.5 and 98.5

2. The product of 127.2 and .0037 is

   A. 4706.4   B. 470.64   C. .47064   D. .0047064

3. The wind velocity at a certain location was measured four times in a 24-hour period. The readings were 32 mph, 10 mph, 16 mph, and 2 mph.
   The AVERAGE wind velocity for that day was _____ mph.

   A. 24   B. 20   C. 15   D. 13

4. When 280 is divided by .014, the answer is

   A. .002   B. 20   C. 200   D. 20,000

5. The square root of 289 is

   A. 1.7   B. 9.7   C. 17   D. 144.5

6. The watts drawn by a resistive load is to be determined. To do this, a voltmeter (10V full scale) is connected across the load, and an ammeter (10 amps full scale) is connected in series with the load. Both instruments are specified as having 1% (full scale) accuracy. The voltmeter reads 9.2V; the ammeter reads 8.3 amps.
   The MOST valid value for the watts drawn is _____ watts.

   A. 76   B. 76.36   C. 76.4   D. 80

7. The formula for converting degrees Centigrade to degrees Fahrenheit is: $°F = (9/5) \cdot (°C) + 32$.
   A temperature of 25° C is equal to

   A. 102.6° F   B. 85° F   C. 77° F   D. 43° F

8. The prefix *kilo* means

   A. multiply by one million
   B. divide by one million
   C. multiply by one thousand
   D. divide by one hundred

9. 2^8 is equal to

   A. 512   B. 256   C. 124   D. 82

10. The prefix *milli* means

    A. multiply by 100
    B. divide by one thousand
    C. divide by one million
    D. multiply by one million

11. If 1/X = 1/20 + 1/20 + 1/40, the value of X is

    A. .125 B. 8 C. 16 D. 20

12. 2×10^6 multiplied by 4×10^{-6} equals

    A. 8 B. 8×10^{-12} C. 8×10^{12} D. 8×10^3

13. 1 inch equals _____ cm.

    A. 0.62 B. 2.54 C. 3.94 D. 16.2

14. 1 kg equals

    A. 2.2 lbs. B. 17.3 oz. C. 0.52 lbs. D. 12 oz.

15. 1 liter equals

    A. 3.78 quarts
    B. 1.057 quarts
    C. 1.39 pints
    D. .067 gallons

16. A circle has a radius of 10 inches.
    Its circumference is _____ inches.

    A. 72.3 B. 62.8 C. 31.4 D. 25

17. A right angle triangle has sides measuring 3 inches and 4 inches; its hypotenuse is 5 inches.
    The area of this triangle is _____ square inches.

    A. 6 B. 20 C. 15 D. 60

18. A square has an area of 81 square inches.
    The length of each side is _____ inches.

    A. 7.9 B. 9 C. 11 D. 17

19. A bottle contains 11 pints of liquid. To this bottle 1.32 pints is then added.
    This is an increase of

    A. 6% B. 9% C. 12% D. 16%

20. A week ago a storage battery read 12.4V. Today its voltage is 8.1% less.
    Its voltage is now

    A. 11.4 B. 10.8 C. 9.3 D. 10.2

21. The advantage of a vacuum tube voltmeter over a regular voltmeter is that it

    A. operates on batteries
    B. operates on 120V AC
    C. has a low input impedance
    D. has a high input impedance

22. A g_m tube tester measures a vacuum tube's

    A. capacitance
    B. resistance
    C. emission
    D. transconductance

23. A cathode ray tube is used in a(n)

    A. audio amplifier
    B. radio frequency amplifier
    C. oscilloscope
    D. volt-ohm-milliammeter

24. A voltmeter is described as having *1000 ohms per volt*. The current required to produce full scale deflection is

    A. 1 milliampere
    B. 1 ampere
    C. 20 milliamperes
    D. 0.05 milliamperes

25. The PRIMARY use of a test oscilloscope is to

    A. analyze complex waveforms
    B. measure resistance
    C. measure capacitance
    D. measure DC voltages

26. A spectrophotometer is an instrument that measures

    A. photographic film density
    B. the amount of light of a particular wavelength
    C. the amount of airborne dust
    D. x-ray radiation

27. The test instrument generally known as a *multitester* will measure, among other things,

    A. temperature
    B. beta radiation
    C. AC watts
    D. DC milliamperes

28. A lightmeter used in measuring incident light gives readings in

    A. footcandles
    B. candlepower
    C. lumens
    D. foot-lamberts

29. A selenium photocell is a type known as photo-

    A. emissive
    B. resistive
    C. voltaic
    D. transistive

30. In wiring electronic circuits, the solder GENERALLY used is _____ solder.

    A. silver
    B. acid core
    C. aluminum
    D. rosin core

31. An unconscious victim of electric shock should be orally administered

    A. nothing
    B. coffee
    C. alcohol
    D. aromatic apirits of ammonia

32. Persons operating x-ray equipment should wear

   A. safety goggles
   B. insulating gloves
   C. a lead-coated apron and gloves
   D. a surgical mask

33. Harmful radiation is emitted by the element

   A. neon   B. lithium   C. platinum   D. radium

34. When a victim of electrical shock or near drowning is given artificial respiration and he does not appear to respond, the treatment should continue for at least

   A. four hours   B. fifteen minutes
   C. five minutes   D. fifteen hours

35. A person maintaining high voltage equipment should avoid wearing

   A. long hair
   B. sneakers
   C. rings and metallic watchbands
   D. eyeglasses

36. Portable AC equipment is often equipped with a three-wire cable and a three-prong male plug.
   The reason for this is to prevent

   A. radiation   B. electric shock
   C. oscillation   D. ground currents

37. Smoke is seen issuing from a piece of electronic equipment. The FIRST thing that should be done is to

   A. call the fire department
   B. pour water on it
   C. look for a fire extinguisher
   D. shut off the power

38. A match should not be used when inspecting the electrolyte level in a lead-acid battery because the cells emit

   A. nitrogen   B. hydrogen
   C. carbon dioxide   D. sulfur dioxide

39. A person feels nauseated, his mental capacity has been lowered, and he has a severe throbbing headache. It is suspected that he has been poisoned by gas, but there is no apparent odor.
   The poisonous gas is MOST likely to be

   A. sulfur dioxide   B. hydrogen cyanide
   C. carbon monoxide   D. chlorine

40. The purpose of an interlock on a piece of electronic equipment is to

   A. prevent theft of the vacuum tubes
   B. prevent electrical shock to maintenance personnel
   C. prevent rf radiation
   D. keep the equipment cool

41. An alternating voltage is applied to an inductance.
    As the frequency of the voltage is decreased, the impedance of the inductance

   A. decreases
   B. increases
   C. follows the alternating voltage
   D. remains the same

42. A 0.25 ufd condenser is connected in parallel with a 0.50 ufd condenser.
    The resultant capacity is _____ ufd.

   A. 0.167   B. 0.37   C. 0.75   D. 2.5

43. The electrolyte in a carbon-zinc dry cell is

   A. sulfuric acid   B. ammonium chloride
   C. lithium chloride   D. sodium chloride

44. A 5000-ohm resistor has a voltage of 25 volts applied to it.
    The current drawn by the resistor is

   A. 5 milliamperes   B. 5 amperes
   C. 75 milliamperes   D. 1.25 milliamperes

45. A certain resistor has three colored bands around it.
    The one nearest the end is red, the next one is gray, and the next one is yellow.
    The value of the resistor is

   A. 2.7 megaohms   B. 280,000 ohms
   C. 3270 ohms   D. 449 ohms

Questions 46-50.

DIRECTIONS: Questions 46 through 50 are to be answered on the basis of the following paragraph.

The second half of the twin triode acts as a phase modulator. The rf output of the crystal oscillator is impressed on the phase-modulator grid by means of a blocking condenser. The cathode circuit is provided with a large amount of degeneration by an un-bypassed cathode resistor. Because of this degenerative feedback, the transconductance of the triode is abnormally low, so low that the plate current is affected as much by the direct grid-plate capacitance as by the transconductance. The two effects result in plate current vectors almost 180° apart, and the total plate current is the resultant of the two components. In phase, it will be about 90° removed from the phase of the voltage impressed on the grid.

46. As used in the above paragraph, the word *impressed* means MOST NEARLY 46.____

   A. applied   B. blocked   C. changed   D. detached

47. As used in the above paragraph, the word *components* refers to the 47.____

   A. blocking condenser and cathode resistor
   B. twin triode
   C. plate current vectors
   D. grid-plate capacitance

48. According to the above paragraph, degenerative feedback is obtained by means of 48.____

   A. a crystal oscillator
   B. the plate voltage
   C. an un-bypassed cathode resistor
   D. a blocking condenser

49. According to the above paragraph, the cathode resistor is 49.____

   A. very large
   B. not bypassed
   C. in series with an inductance
   D. shunted by a blocking condenser

50. According to the above paragraph, the phase angle between the grid voltage and the total plate current is APPROXIMATELY 50.____

   A. 180°   B. 90°   C. 270°   D. zero

KEY (CORRECT ANSWERS)

1. B	11. B	21. D	31. A	41. A
2. C	12. C	22. D	32. C	42. C
3. C	13. B	23. C	33. D	43. B
4. D	14. A	24. A	34. A	44. A
5. C	15. B	25. A	35. C	45. B
6. A	16. B	26. B	36. B	46. A
7. C	17. A	27. D	37. D	47. C
8. C	18. B	28. A	38. B	48. C
9. B	19. C	29. C	39. C	49. B
10. B	20. A	30. D	40. B	50. B

HIGHWAY TRAFFIC SIGNALS

CONTENTS

	Page

A. General

Section A- 1. Types ... 1
A- 2. Basis of Installation ... 1

B. Traffic Control Signals

Section B- 1. General Aspects ... 1
B- 2. Area of Control ... 1
B- 3. Advantages and Disadvantages of Traffic Control Signals ... 2
B- 4. Portable Traffic Control Signals ... 2
B- 5. Meaning of Signal Indications ... 2
B- 6. Application of Signal Indications ... 4
B- 7. Number of Lenses per Signal Face ... 6
B- 8. Size and Design of Signal Lenses ... 6
B- 9. Arrangement of Lenses in Signal Faces ... 7
B-10. Illumination of Lenses ... 9
B-11. Visibility and Shielding of Signal Faces ... 10
B-12. Number and Locations of Signal Faces ... 10
B-13. Height of Signal Faces ... 13
B-14. Transverse Location of Traffic Signal Supports and Controller Cabinets ... 13
B-15. Vehicle Change Interval ... 14
B-16. Unexpected Conflicts During Green Interval ... 14
B-17. Coordination of Traffic Control Signals ... 15
B-18. Flashing Operation of Traffic Control Signals ... 15
B-19. Continuity of Operation ... 16
B-20. Signal Operation Must Relate to Traffic Flow ... 16
B-21. Traffic Signals Near Grade Crossings ... 16
B-22. Emergency Operation of Traffic Signals ... 17
B-23. Maintenance of Traffic Control Signals ... 18
B-24. Painting ... 19
B-25. Vehicle Detectors ... 19
B-26. Auxiliary Signs ... 19
B-27. Removal of Confusing Advertising Lights ... 20

94

HIGHWAY TRAFFIC SIGNALS

A. GENERAL

A-1 Types

This part relates to a group of devices called highway traffic signals. These devices include: traffic control signals, beacons, lane-use control signals, drawbridge signals, emergency traffic control signals and train approach signals and gates. Only the first of these will be discussed in this section.

A-2 Basis of Installation

In most cases the installation of a highway traffic control signal will operate either to the advantage or disadvantage of the vehicles and persons controlled. A careful analysis of traffic operations and other factors at a large number of signalized and unsignalized intersections, coupled with the judgment of experienced engineers, have provided a series of warrants that define the minimum conditions under which signal installations may be justified. Consequently the selection and use of this control device should be preceded by a thorough engineering study of roadway and traffic conditions.

Engineering studies should be made of operating signals to determine if the type of installation and the timing program meet the current requirements of traffic.

B. TRAFFIC CONTROL SIGNALS

B-1 General Aspects

There are two types of traffic control signals, pretimed and traffic-actuated.

The features of traffic control signals in which vehicle operators and pedestrians are interested are the location, design, indications, and legal significance of the signals. These are identical for all types of traffic control signals. Uniformity in the design features that affect the traffic to be controlled (as set forth in this Manual) is especially important for safe and efficient traffic operations.

Special police supervision and/or enforcement should be provided for a new non-intersection location.

B-2 Area of Control

A traffic control signal shall control traffic only at the intersection or mid-block location where the installation is placed.

B-3 Advantages and Disadvantages of Traffic Control Signals

Traffic control signals are valuable devices for the control of vehicle and pedestrian traffic. However, because they assign the right-of-way to the various traffic movements, traffic control signals exert a profound influence on traffic flow.

Traffic control signals, properly located and operated usually have one or more of the following advantages:

1. They can provide for the orderly movement of traffic.
2. Where proper physical layouts and control measures are used, they can increase the traffic-handling capacity of the intersection.
3. They can reduce the frequency of certain types of accidents, especially the right-angle type.
4. Under favorable conditions, they can be coordinated to provide for continuous or nearly continuous movement of traffic at a definite speed along a given route.
5. They can be used to interrupt heavy traffic at intervals to permit other traffic, vehicular or pedestrian, to cross.

Many laymen believe that traffic signals provide the solution to all traffic problems at intersections. This has led to their installation at a large number of locations where no legitimate factual warrant exists.

Traffic signal installations, even though warranted by traffic and roadway conditions, can be ill-designed, ineffectively placed, improperly operated, or poorly maintained. The following factors can result from improper or unwarranted signal installations:

1. Excessive delay may be caused.
2. Disobedience of the signal indications is encouraged.
3. The use of less adequate routes may be induced in an attempt to avoid such signals.
4. Accident frequency (especially the rear-end type) can be significantly increased.

B-4 Portable Traffic Control Signals

A portable traffic control signal not meeting all the requirements is not recognized as a standard traffic control device.

B-5 Meaning of Signal Indications

The following meanings shall be given to highway traffic signal indications, except those on pedestrian signals:

1. Green indications shall have the following meanings:

   a. Traffic, except pedestrians, facing a CIRCULAR GREEN may proceed straight through or turn right or left unless a sign at such place prohibits either such turn. But vehicular traffic, including vehicles turning right or left, shall yield the right-of-way to other vehicles, and to pedestrians lawfully within the intersection or an adjacent crosswalk, at the time such signal is exhibited.

b. Traffic, except pedestrians, facing a GREEN ARROW, shown alone or in combination with another indication, may cautiously enter the intersection only to make the movement indicated by such arrow, or such other movement as is permitted by other indications shown at the same time. Such vehicular traffic shall yield the right-of-way to pedestrians lawfully within an adjacent crosswalk and to other traffic lawfully using the intersection.

c. Unless otherwise directed by a pedestrian signal, pedestrians facing any green indication, except when the sole green indication is a turn arrow, may proceed across the roadway within any marked or unmarked crosswalk.

2. Steady yellow indications shall have the following meanings:

a. Traffic, except pedestrians, facing a steady CIRCULAR YELLOW or YELLOW ARROW signal is thereby warned that the related green movement is being terminated or that a red indication will be exhibited immediately thereafter when vehicular traffic shall not enter the intersection.

b. Pedestrians facing a steady CIRCULAR YELLOW or YELLOW ARROW signal, unless otherwise directed by a pedestrian signal, are thereby advised that there is insufficient time to cross the roadway before a red indication is shown and no pedestrian shall then start to cross the roadway.

3. Steady red indications shall have the following meanings:

a. Traffic, except pedestrians, facing a steady CIRCULAR RED signal alone shall stop at a clearly marked stop line, but if none, before entering the crosswalk on the near side of the intersection, or if none, then before entering the intersection and shall remain standing until an indication to proceed is shown except as provided in b below.

b. When a sign is in place permitting a turn, traffic, except pedestrians, facing a steady CIRCULAR RED signal may cautiously enter the intersection to make the turn indicated by such sign after stopping as provided in a above. Such vehicular traffic shall yield the right-of-way to pedestrians lawfully within an adjacent crosswalk and to other traffic lawfully using the intersection.

c. Unless otherwise directed by a pedestrian signal, pedestrians facing a steady CIRCULAR RED signal alone shall not enter the roadway.

d. Traffic, except pedestrians, facing a steady RED ARROW indication may not enter the intersection to make the movement indicated by such arrow, and unless entering the intersection to make such other movement as is permitted by other indications shown at the same time, shall stop at a clearly marked stop line, but if none, before entering the crosswalk on the near side of the intersection, or if none, then before entering the intersection and shall remain standing until an indication to make the movement indicated by such arrow is shown.

e. Unless otherwise directed by a pedestrian signal, pedestrians facing a steady RED ARROW signal indication shall not enter the roadway.

4. Flashing signal indications shall have the following meanings:

a. Flashing red (stop signal)—When a red lens is illuminated with rapid intermittent flashes, drivers of vehicles shall stop at a clearly marked stop line, but if none, before entering the crosswalk on the near side of the intersection, or if none, then at the point nearest the intersecting roadway where the driver has a view of approaching traffic on the intersecting roadway before entering the intersection, and the right to proceed shall be subject to the rules applicable after making a stop at a STOP sign.

b. Flashing yellow (caution signal)—When a yellow lens is illuminated with rapid intermittent flashes, drivers of vehicles may proceed through the intersection or past such signal only with caution.

B-6 Application of Signal Indications

Basic displays used in signal operations are the steady CIRCULAR RED, CIRCULAR YELLOW or CIRCULAR GREEN indication, used on each of the approaches. The application for these signal indications shall be as follows:

1. A steady CIRCULAR RED indication:

a. Shall be given when it is intended to prohibit traffic from entering the intersection or other controlled area.

b. Should be displayed with the appropriate green arrow indications when it is intended to permit traffic to make a specified turn or turns, and to prohibit traffic from proceeding straight ahead through the controlled area. This display is optional where it is physically impossible for traffic to go straight ahead, as at the head of a "T" intersection.

c. Shall be given when it is intended to prohibit all traffic, except pedestrians directed by a pedestrian signal, from entering the intersection or other controlled area.

2. A steady CIRCULAR YELLOW indication:

a. Shall be given following a CIRCULAR GREEN indication in the same signal face.

b. Is an optional alternative to a yellow arrow indication following a green arrow indication in a separate signal face used exclusively to control a single directional movement.

3. A steady CIRCULAR GREEN indication shall be given only when it is intended to permit traffic to proceed in any direction which is lawful and practical.

4. Steady RED ARROW, YELLOW ARROW and GREEN ARROW indications may be used in lieu of the corresponding circular indications at the following locations:

a. On an approach intersecting a one-way street.

b. Where certain movements are prohibited.

c. Where certain movements are physically impossible.

d. On an intersection approach which has an exclusive lane for turning movements.

e. Where turning movements are "protected" from conflicting movements by other indications or by the signal sequence.

f. Where all the movements on the approach do not begin or end at the same time and where the indications for the turning movements will also be visible to traffic with other allowable movements.

If steady arrow indications are used:

a. A steady RED ARROW indication shall be used only in a separate signal face which also contains steady YELLOW ARROW and GREEN ARROW indications. It shall be used for controlling only a single traffic movement.

b. A steady YELLOW ARROW indication shall be used following a GREEN ARROW indication (which has been displayed simultaneously with a CIRCULAR RED indication in the same signal face).

c. A steady YELLOW ARROW indication may be used (in a separate signal face) following a GREEN ARROW indication, when that face is used exclusively to control a single directional movement.

d. A steady YELLOW ARROW indication may be used to indicate the clearance interval following the termination of a GREEN ARROW indication (when displayed simultaneously with a continuing CIRCULAR GREEN indication in the same signal face).

e. A steady GREEN ARROW indication shall be used only when there would be no conflict with other vehicles or with pedestrians crossing in conformance with the WALK indication.

5. The following combinations of signal indications shall not be simultaneously displayed on any one signal face, and shall not be simultaneously displayed in different signal faces on any one approach to an intersection unless the signal faces are shielded, hooded, louvered, positioned or designed so that none of these prohibited combinations of signal indications is readily visible to drivers:

    a. CIRCULAR GREEN with CIRCULAR YELLOW.

    b. Straight-through GREEN ARROW with CIRCULAR RED.

    c. CIRCULAR RED with CIRCULAR YELLOW.

    d. CIRCULAR GREEN with CIRCULAR RED.

    e. CIRCULAR GREEN with RED ARROW.

6. When a traffic control signal is put on flashing operation, normally a yellow indication should be used for the major street and a red indication for the other approaches. Yellow indications shall not be used for all approaches. The following applications shall apply whenever signals are placed in flashing operation:

    a. A CIRCULAR YELLOW indication shall be flashed instead of any YELLOW ARROW indication which may be included in that signal face.

    b. No CIRCULAR GREEN or GREEN ARROW indication or flashing yellow indication shall be terminated and immediately followed by a steady red or flashing red indication without the display of the steady yellow change indication; however, transition may be made directly from a CIRCULAR GREEN or GREEN ARROW indication to a flashing yellow indication.

B-7 Number of Lenses per Signal Face

Each signal face, except in pedestrian signals, shall have at least three lenses, but not more than five. The lenses shall be red, yellow or green in color, and shall give a circular or arrow type of indication. Allowable exceptions to the above are:

1. Where a single section green arrow lens is used alone to indicate a continuous movement.

2. As discussed under Unexpected Conflicts During Green Interval (sec. B-16).

3. Where one or more indications are repeated for reasons of safety or impact.

B-8 Size and Design of Signal Lenses

The aspect of all signal lenses, except in pedestrian signals, shall be circular. There shall be two sizes for lenses, 8 inches and 12 inches nominal diameter.

Twelve-inch lenses normally should be used:

1. For intersections with 85 percentile approach speeds exceeding 40 mph.

2. For intersections where signalization might be unexpected.

3. For special problem locations, such as those with conflicting or competing background lighting.

4. For intersections where drivers may view both traffic control and lane-direction-control signs simultaneously.

5. For all arrow indications.

Arrows shall be pointed vertically upward to indicate a straight-through movement and in a horizontal direction to indicate a turn at approximately right angles. When the angle of the turn is substantially different from a right angle, the arrow should be positioned on an upward slope at an angle approximately equal to that of the turn.

Each arrow lens shall show only one arrow direction. The arrow shall be the only illuminated part of the lens visible.

In no case shall letters or numbers be displayed as part of a vehicular signal indication.

Except for the requirements of this section, all lenses shall conform to the Standard for Adjustable Face Vehicle Traffic Control Signal Heads, 1970 Edition.

B-9 Arrangement of Lenses in Signal Faces

The lenses in a signal face shall be arranged in a vertical or horizontal straight line, except that in a vertical array, lenses of the same color may be arranged horizontally adjacent to each other at right angles to the basic straight line arrangement (fig. 4-1). Such clusters shall be limited to two identical lenses or to two or three different lenses of the same color.

In each signal face, all red lenses in vertical signals shall be located above, and in horizontal signals shall be located to the left of all yellow and green lenses.

A CIRCULAR YELLOW lens shall be located between the red lens or lenses and all other lenses.

In vertically arranged signal faces, each YELLOW ARROW lens shall be located immediately above the GREEN ARROW lens to which it applies. In horizontally arranged signals, the YELLOW ARROW shall be located immediately to the left of the GREEN ARROW lens.

8

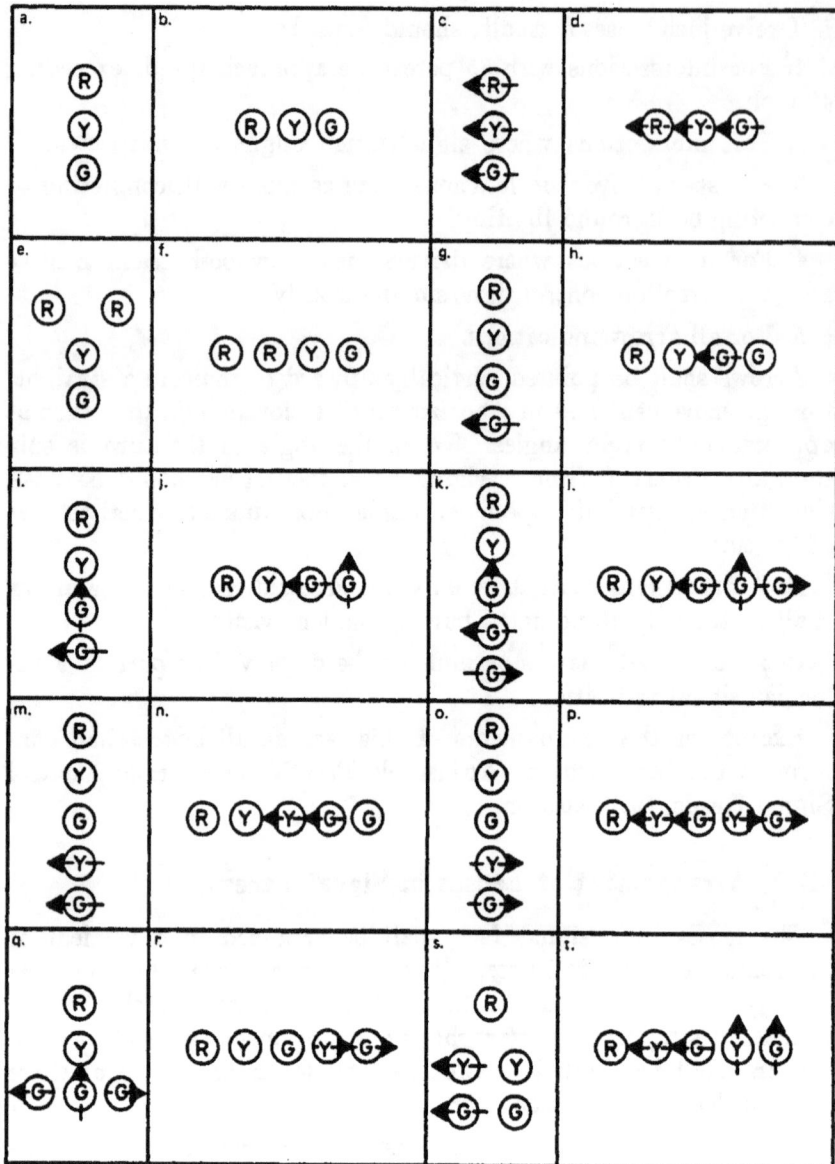

Figure 1. Typical arrangements of lenses in signal faces.

The relative positions of lenses within the signal face shall be as follows:

1. In a vertical signal face from top to bottom:
    CIRCULAR RED
    Left turn RED ARROW
    Right turn RED ARROW
    CIRCULAR YELLOW

    Straight through YELLOW ARROW
    Straight through GREEN ARROW
    CIRCULAR GREEN
    Left turn YELLOW ARROW
    Left turn GREEN ARROW
    Right turn YELLOW ARROW
    Right turn GREEN ARROW

2. In a horizontal signal face from left to right:
    CIRCULAR RED
    Left turn RED ARROW
    Right turn RED ARROW
    CIRCULAR YELLOW
    Left turn YELLOW ARROW
    Left turn GREEN ARROW
    CIRCULAR GREEN
    Straight through YELLOW ARROW
    Straight through GREEN ARROW
    Right turn YELLOW ARROW
    Right turn GREEN ARROW

3. In a cluster, identical signal indications may be repeated in adjacent vertical or horizontal locations within the same signal face. If adjacent indications in a cluster are not identical, their arrangement shall follow paragraph 1 or 2 above, as applicable.

Basic horizontal and vertical display faces may be used on the same approach provided they are separated to meet the lateral clearance required in section B–12.

Figure 1 shows some possible arrangements of lenses in signal faces.

B–10 Illumination of Lenses

Each signal lens shall be illuminated independently.

When a signal lens, except in a pedestrian signal, is illuminated and the view of such an indication is not otherwise physically obstructed, it shall be clearly visible (to drivers it controls) for a distance of a least ¼ mile under normal atmospheric conditions.

The intensity and distribution of light from each illuminated signal lens should conform to the Standard for Adjustable Face Vehicle Traffic Control Signal Heads, Revised 1970; and the Standard for Traffic Signal Lamps, December 1967.

When 12″ lens signals with 150 watt lamps are placed on flashing for nighttime operation and the flashing yellow indication is so bright as to cause excessive glare, an automatic dimming device should be used to reduce the brilliance of the flashing 12″ yellow.

B-11 Visibility and Shielding of Signal Faces

Each signal face shall be so adjusted that its indications will be of maximum effectiveness to the approaching traffic for which they are intended.

Visors should be used on all signal faces to aid in directing the signal indication specifically to approaching traffic, as well as to reduce "sun phantom" resulting from external light entering the lens. Back-plates normally should be used on one-way and back-to-back two-way overhead signals, and when one signal face controls a movement.

In general, vehicular signal faces should be aimed to have maximum effectiveness for an approaching driver located a distance from the stop line equal to the distance traversed while stopping. This distance should include that covered while reacting to the signal as well as that covered while bringing the vehicle to a stop from an average approach speed. The influence of curves, grades, and obstructions should be considered in directing and locating signals.

Irregular street design frequently necessitates placing signals for different street approaches with a comparatively small angle between their indications. In these cases, each signal indication shall, to the extent practicable, be shielded or directed by visors, louvers, or other means so that an approaching driver can see only the indication controlling his movement. Tunnel visors exceeding 12" in length shall not be used on free-swinging signals.

The foregoing does not preclude the use of special signal faces such that the driver does not see their indications before seeing other indications further ahead, when simultaneous viewing of both signal indications could cause the driver to be misdirected.

B-12 Number and Location of Signal Faces

The primary consideration in signal face placement shall be visibility. Drivers approaching a signalized intersection or other signalized area, such as a mid-block crosswalk, shall be given a clear and unmistakable indication of their right-of-way assignment. Critical elements are lateral and vertical angles of sight toward a signal face, as determined by typical driver eye position, vehicle design, and the vertical, longitudinal and lateral position of the signal face. The geometry of each intersection to be signalized, including vertical grades and horizontal curves, should be considered in signal face placement.

The visibility, location and number of signal faces for each approach to an intersection or a mid-block crosswalk shall be as follows:

1. A minimum of two signal faces for through-traffic shall be provided and should be continuously visible from a point at least the following distances in advance of and to the stop line, unless physical obstruction of their visibility exists:

85 Percentile Speed	Minimum Visibility Distance (Ft.)
20	100
25	175
30	250
35	325
40	400
45	475
50	550
55	625
60	700

2. Where physical conditions prevent drivers from having a continuous view of at least two signal indications as specified herein, a suitable sign shall be erected to warn approaching traffic. It may be supplemented by a Hazard Identification Beacon.
A beacon utilized in this manner may be interconnected with the traffic signal controller in such a manner as to flash yellow during the period when drivers passing this beacon, at the legal speed for the roadway, may encounter a red signal upon arrival at the signalized location.

3. A single signal face is permissible for the control of an exclusive turn lane. Such a signal face shall be in addition to the minimum of two signal faces for through-traffic. When the indications of a separate signal face or faces controlling an exclusive turn lane will also be visible to traffic with other allowable movements, a sign LEFT (or RIGHT) TURN SIGNAL shall be located adjacent to such signal face. When the face consists entirely of arrow indications, such a sign is not required.

4. Except where the width of the intersecting street or other conditions make it physically impractical, at least one and preferably both of the signal faces required by paragraph (1) above shall be located not less than 40 feet nor more than 120 feet beyond the stop line. Where both of the signal faces required by paragraph (1) above are post-mounted, they shall both be on the far side of the intersection, one on the right and one on the left or on the median island if practical. The signal face required by paragraph (3) above shall conform to the same location requirements as the signal faces required by paragraph (1) to the extent practical.

5. Except where the width of the intersecting street or other conditions make it physically impractical, at least one and preferably

both of the signal faces required by paragraph (1) above shall be located between two lines intersecting with the center of the approach lanes at the stop line, one making an angle of approximately 20 degrees to the right of the center of the approach extended, and the other making an angle of approximately 20 degrees to the left of the center of the approach extended (fig. 2).

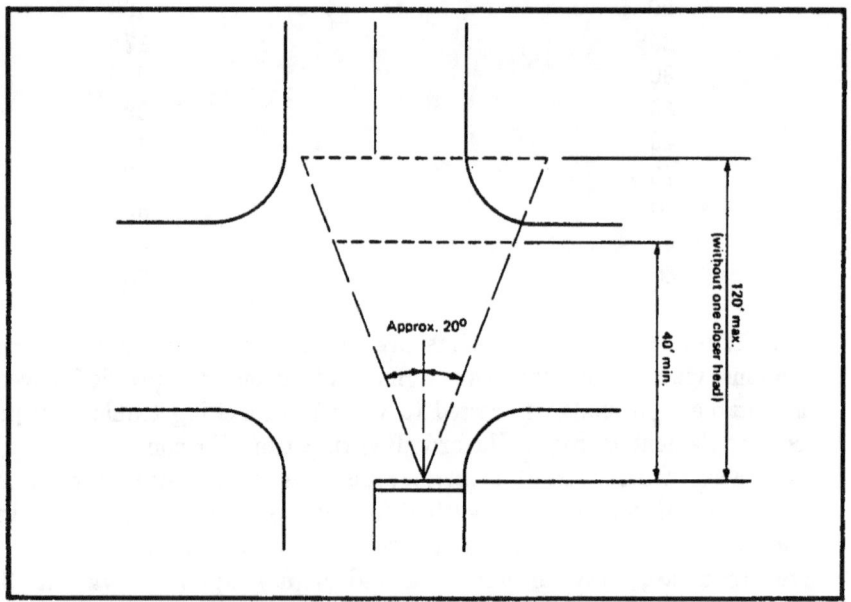

Figure 2. Desirable location of signal faces.

6. Near-side signals should be located as near as practicable to the stop line.

7. Where a signal face controls a specific lane or lanes of approach, its transverse position should be unmistakably in line with the path of that movement.

8. Required signal faces for any one approach shall be not less than eight feet apart measured horizontally between centers of faces.

9. When the nearest signal face is more than 120 feet beyond the stop line, a supplemental near side signal indication shall be provided.

10. A signal face mounted on a span wire or mast arm should be located as near as practicable to the line of the driver's normal view.

11. Supplemental signal faces should be used when an engineering study has shown that they are needed to achieve both advance and immediate intersection visibility. When used, they should be lo-

cated to provide optimum visibility for the movement to be controlled. The following limitations apply:

a. Left turn arrows shall not be used in near-right faces.

b. Right turn arrows shall not be used in far-left faces. A far-side median mount signal shall be considered as a far-left signal for this application.

At signalized mid-block crosswalks, there should be at least one signal face over the traveled roadway for each approach. In other respects, a traffic control signal at a mid-block location shall meet the requirements set forth herein.

The transverse location of a signal face, shall, if mounted on the top of a post or on a short bracket from it, conform with section B-14.

Supplementary pedestrian signals shall be used where warranted,

B-13 Height of Signal Faces

The bottom of the housing of a signal face, not mounted over a roadway, shall not be less than 8 feet nor more than 15 feet above the sidewalk or, if none, above the pavement grade at the center of the highway.

The bottom of the housing of a signal face suspended over a roadway shall not be less than 15 feet nor more than 19 feet above the pavement grade at the center of the roadway.

Within the above limits, optimum visibility and adequate clearance should be the guiding considerations in deciding signal height. Grades on approaching streets may be important factors, and should be considered in determining the most appropriate height.

B-14 Transverse Location of Traffic Signal Supports and Controller Cabinets

In the placement of signal supports, primary consideration shall be given to ensuring the proper visibility of signal faces as described in sections B-12 and 13. However, in the interest of safety, signal supports and controller cabinets should be placed as far as practicable from the edge of the traveled way without adversely affecting signal visibility.

Supports for post-mounted signal heads at the side of a street with curbs shall have a horizontal clearance of not less than two feet from the face of a vertical curb. Where there is no curb, supports for post-mounted signal heads shall have a horizontal clearance of not less than two feet from the edge of a shoulder, within the limits of normal vertical clearance. A signal support should not obstruct a crosswalk.

No part of a concrete base for a signal support should extend more than 4 inches above the ground level at any point, except that this limitation does not apply to the concrete base for a rigid (non-breakaway) support.

On medians, the above minimum clearances for signal supports should be obtained where practicable. Any supports which cannot be located with the required clearances should be of the breakaway type or should be guarded if at all practicable.

B-15 Vehicle Change Interval

A yellow vehicle change interval shall be used following each CIRCULAR GREEN interval and, where applicable after each GREEN ARROW interval. In no case shall a CIRCULAR YELLOW indication be displayed in conjunction with the change from CIRCULAR RED to CIRCULAR GREEN. Separate signal faces should be used when exclusive turning movements are controlled by GREEN ARROWS (sec. B-6).

The exclusive function of the steady yellow interval shall be to warn traffic of an impending change in the right-of-way assignment.

Yellow vehicle change intervals should have a range of approximately 3 to 6 seconds. Generally the longer intervals are appropriate to higher approach speeds.

The yellow vehicle change interval may be followed by a short all-way red clearance interval, of sufficient duration to permit the intersection to clear before cross traffic is released.

A clearance interval shall be provided between the termination of a GREEN ARROW indication and the showing of a green indication to any conflicting traffic movement.

B-16 Unexpected Conflicts During Green Interval

No movement that may involve an unexpected crossing of pathways of moving traffic should be indicated during any green interval, except when:

1. The movement involves only slight hazard;
2. Serious traffic delays are materially reduced by permitting the conflicting movement; and
3. Drivers and pedestrians subjected to the unexpected conflict are effectively warned thereof.

When such conditions of possible unexpected conflict exist, warning may be given by a sign or, by the use of an appropriate signal indication as set forth in section B-7. The foregoing applies to vehicle-pedestrian conflicts as well as to vehicle-vehicle conflicts.

B-17 Coordination of Traffic Control Signals

Traffic control signals within one-half of a mile of one another along a major route or in a network of intersecting major routes should be operated in coordination, preferably with interconnected controllers. However, coordination need not be maintained across boundaries between signal systems which operate on different time cycles. Coordinated operation normally should include both pretimed signals and traffic-actuated signals within the appropriate distances.

For coordination with railroad grade crossings signals see section B-21.

B-18 Flashing Operation of Traffic Control Signals

All traffic signal installations shall be provided with an electrical flashing mechanism supplementary to the signal timer. A manual switch, or where appropriate, automatic means, shall be provided to actuate the flashing mechanism. The signal timer shall be removable without affecting the flashing operation. The mechanism shall operate in a manner similar to that of an Intersection Control Beacon to provide intermittent illumination of selected signal lenses.

The illuminating element in a flashing signal shall be flashed continuously at a rate of not less than 50 nor more than 60 times per minute. The illuminated period of each flash shall be not less than half and not more than two-thirds of the total flash cycle.

When traffic control signals are put on flashing operation, the signal indications given to the several streets shall be as specified in section B-6.

Automatic changes from flashing to stop-and-go operation shall be made at the beginning of the major street green interval, preferably at the beginning of the common major street green interval, (i.e., when a green indication is shown in both directions on the major street). Automatic changes from stop-and-go to flashing operation shall be made at the end of the common major street red interval, (i.e., when a red indication is shown in both directions on the major street).

The change from the flashing to stop-and-go operation, or from stop-and-go to flashing operation by manual switch may be made at any time.

Where there is no common major street green interval, the automatic change from flashing to stop-and-go operation shall be made at the beginning of the green interval for the major traffic movement on the major street. It may be necessary to provide a short, steady all-red interval for the other approaches before changing from flashing yellow or flashing red to green on the major approach.

B-19 Continuity of Operation

A traffic signal installation, except as provided below, shall be operated as a stop-and-go device or as a flashing device.

When a signal installation is not in operation such as prior to placing it in service, during seasonal shutdowns, or when it is not desirable to operate the signals, they should be hooded, turned or taken down to clearly indicate that the signal is not in operation.

When a traffic signal installation is being operated in the usual (stop-and-go) manner, at least one indication in each signal face shall be illuminated.

When a traffic signal installation is being operated as a flashing device, the yellow indication shall be flashed in at least two required signal faces (sec. B-12) on each approach on which traffic is not stopped and the red indication shall be flashed in at least two required signal faces (sec. B-12) on each approach on which traffic is required to stop.

The above provisions do not apply to emergency-traffic signals or draw-bridge signals.

When a single-section, continuously illuminated GREEN ARROW lens is used alone to indicate a continuous movement, it may be continuously illuminated when the other signal indications in the signal installation are flashed.

B-20 Signal Operation Must Relate to Traffic Flow

Traffic control signals shall be operated in a manner consistent with traffic requirements. Data from engineering studies shall be used to determine the proper phasing and timing for a signal.

Since traffic flows and patterns change, it is necessary that the engineering data be updated and re-evaluated regularly.

To assure that the approved operating pattern including timing is displayed to the driver, regular checks including the use of accurate timing devices should be made.

B-21 Traffic Signals Near Grade Crossings

When a railroad grade crossing, protected by train-approach signals is within or near an intersection controlled by a traffic control signal, the control of the traffic signal should be preempted from the signal controller upon approach of trains to avoid conflicting aspects of the traffic signal and the train-approach signal. This preemption feature requires a closed electrical circuit between the control relay of the train-approach signals and the preemptor in order to establish and maintain the preempted condition during the time that the train-approach signals are in operation. Except under unusual circumstances, the interconnection should be limited to the traffic signals within 200 feet of the crossing.

Traffic control signals shall not be used on mainline railroad crossings in lieu of railroad grade crossing protection devices. However, at industrial track crossings and other places where train movements are very slow (as in switching operations), traffic control signals may be used in lieu of conventional train-approach signals to warn motorists of the approach or presence of a train. The provisions of this part relating to traffic signal design, installation and operation are applicable as appropriate where traffic control signals are so used.

At crossings where train movements are regulated or limited to the extent that train-approach signals are not required, preemption of the adjacent signalized intersections may be desirable to permit non-conflicting highway traffic to proceed during the time the crossing is blocked by a train. Except under unusual circumstances, the interconnection should be limited to the traffic signals within 200 feet of the crossing.

The preemption sequence initiated when the train first enters the approach circuit, shall at once bring into effect a signal display which will permit all vehicles to clear the tracks before the train reaches the intersection or any approach thereto.

When the green indication is preempted by train operation, a yellow change interval must be inserted in the signal sequence in the interest of safety and consistency. To avoid misinterpretation during the time that the clear-out signals are green, consideration should be given to the use of 12-inch red lenses in the signals which govern movement over the tracks (sec. B-8).

After the track clearance phase, the traffic control signal may be operated to permit vehicle movements that do not cross the tracks, but in all cases shall prohibit movements over the tracks.

Where feasible the location and the normal (no trains involved) phasing and timing of traffic control signals near railroad grade crossings should be designed so that vehicles are not required to stop on the tracks even though in some cases this will increase the waiting time. The exact nature of the display and the location of the signals to accomplish this will depend on the physical relationship of the tracks to the intersection area.

When the train clears the crossing it is necessary to return the signal to a designated phase, normally the traffic movement crossing the tracks.

As used herein, the terms "train" and "railroad" shall include transit vehicles operating upon stationary rails or tracks on private right-of-way.

B-22 Emergency Operation of Traffic Signals

Systems in which traffic control signals are preempted by emergency vehicles shall operate to permit a normal change interval to take place in the change from green to yellow to red (or flashing red) before arrival of the emergency vehicle at the preempted location. Systems in which traffic control signals are preempted by emergency vehicles shall be designed and installed so as to provide an indication to the driver of any emergency vehicle approaching an intersection when the equipment fails to preempt the traffic signal at that intersection. This indication shall be designed to be given whether the failure results from a prior preemption by an emergency vehicle on the cross street, by a railroad preemption, from equipment malfunction, or from any other cause.

Traffic signals operating in congested areas during emergency conditions should be operated in a manner designed to keep traffic moving. Prolonged all-red or flashing signal sequences are to be avoided.

B-23 Maintenance of Traffic Control Signals

Prior to the installation of any traffic control signal, the responsibility for its maintenance should be clearly established. The responsible agency should provide for the maintenance of the signal and all of its appurtenances in a responsible manner. To this end the agency should:

1. Provide for alternate operation of the signal during a period of failure, either on flash or manually, or by having manual traffic direction by proper authority as may be warranted by traffic volumes or congestion, or by erecting other traffic control devices.
2. Have properly skilled maintenance available without undue delay for all emergency calls, including lamp failures.
3. Provide properly skilled maintenance for all components.
4. Maintain the appearance of the installation in a manner consistent with the intention of this part, with particular emphasis on painting and on cleaning of the optical system.
5. Service equipment and lamps as frequently as experience proves necessary to prevent undue failures.
6. Provide adequate stand-by equipment to minimize the interruption of signal operation due to equipment failure.

Every controller should be kept in effective operation in strict accordance with its predetermined timing schedule.

A careful check of the correctness of time operation of the controller should be made frequently enough to insure its operating in accordance with the planned timing schedule. Timing changes should be made only by authorized persons. A written record should be made of all timing changes.

Controllers should be carefully cleaned and serviced at least as frequently as specified by the manufacturer and more frequently if experience proves it necessary.

B-24 Painting

The insides of visors (hoods) and the entire surface of louvers, and fins, and the front surface of backplates shall have a dull black finish to minimize light reflection to the side of the signals.

To obtain the best possible contrast with the visual background, it is desirable to paint signal head housings highway yellow.

B-25 Vehicle Detectors

The placement of vehicle detectors in relation to the Stop line is a very important factor in the proper operation of traffic actuated signals and should be a factor in signal design.

Where the total entering traffic on one street is more than twice that on the cross street, detectors on the cross street should be placed closer to the stop line than on the main street.

Additional "calling" detectors may be required on lower volume streets to handle traffic entering the street from driveways between the basic detector and the Stop line.

The transverse placement of detectors should be such that vehicles traveling away from the intersection do not register "false-calls." On narrow two-way roadways this may require use of directional detectors.

B-26 Auxiliary Signs

Signal instruction signs used with traffic signals shall be located adjacent to the signal face to which they apply. Minimum clearance of the total assembly shall conform to the provisions of sections A-23 and B-13.

Stop signs shall not be used in conjunction with any signal operation, except:

1. When the indication flashes red at all times or
2. When a minor street or driveway is located within or adjacent to the controlled area, but does not warrant separate signal control due to extremely low potential for conflict.

When used in conjunction with traffic signals, illuminated signs shall be designed and mounted in such a manner as to avoid glare and reflections that seriously detract from the signal indications. The traffic control signal shall be given dominant position and brightness to assure its target priority in the overall display.

Traffic Signal Speed signs may be used to inform drivers of the speed of progression, if this speed is substantially lower than the speed limits in effect on streets in the signal system.

B-27 Removal of Confusing Advertising Lights

There should be legal authority to prohibit the display of any unauthorized sign, signal, marking, or device which interferes with the effectiveness of any official traffic control device. Specific reference is made to Section 11-205, Uniform Vehicle Code—Revised 1968.

GLOSSARY OF TRAFFIC CONTROL TERMS

TABLE OF CONTENTS

	Page
Access Road ... Desire Line	1
Divided Street ... Left Turn Lane	2
Manual Traffic Control ... Passenger Vehicle	3
Passenger (Transit) Volume ... Separate Turning Lane	4
Shoulder ... Traffic Accident	5
Traffic Actuated Controller ... Uninterrupted Flow	6
Vehicle ... Zone (Origin-Destination Studies)	7

GLOSSARY OF TRAFFIC CONTROL TERMS

A

ACCESS ROAD - Public roads, existing or proposed, needed to provide essential access to military installation and facilities, or to industrial installations and facilities in the activities of which there is specific defense interest. Roads within the boundaries of military reservation are excluded from this definition unless such roads have been dedicated to public use and are not subject to closure.

ACCIDENT SPOT MAP - An area or installation map showing the location of vehicle accidents by means of symbols. Symbols may represent accidents classified as to daylight hours, night hours, injury or death.

ANGLE PARKING - Parking where the longitudinal axes of vehicles form an angle with the alignment of the roadway.

C

CENTER LINE - A line marking the center of a roadway between traffic moving in opposite direction.

COLLISION DIAGRAM - A plan of an intersection or section of roadway on which reported accidents are diagramed by means of arrows showing manner of collision.

COMBINED CONDITION AND COLLISION DIAGRAM - A condition diagram upon which the reported accidents are diagramed by means of arrows showing manner of collision.

CONDITION DIAGRAM - A plan of an intersection or section of roadway showing all objects and physical conditions having a bearing on traffic movement and safety at that location. Usually these are scaled drawings.

CORDON COUNTS - A count of all vehicles and persons entering and leaving a district (cordon area) during a designated period of time.

CORDON AREA - The district bounded by the cordon line and included in a cordon count.

CROSSWALK - Any portion of a roadway at an intersection or elsewhere distinctly indicated for pedestrian crossing by lines or other markings on the surface. Also, that part of a roadway at an intersection included within the connections of the lateral lines of the sidewalks on opposite sides of the traffic way measured from the curbs, or in the absence of curbs, from the edges of the traversable roadway.

D

DELAY - The time consumed while traffic or a specified component of traffic is impeded in its movement by some element over which it has no control usually expressed in seconds per vehicle.

DESIRE LINE - A straight line between the point of origin and point of destination of a trip without regard to routes of travel (used in connection with an origin-destination study).

DIVIDED STREET - A two-way road on which traffic in one direction of travel is separated from that in the opposite direction by a directional separator. Such a road has two or more roadways.

E

85 PERCENTILE SPEED - That speed below which 85 percent of the traffic unit's travel, and above which 15 percent travel.

F

FIXED-TIME CONTROLLER - An automatic controller for supervising the operation of traffic control signals in accordance with a predetermined fixed time cycle and divisions thereof.

FIXED-TIME TRAFFIC SIGNAL - A traffic signal operated by a fixed-time controller.

FLASHING BEACON - A section of a standard traffic signal head, or a similar type device, having a yellow or red lens in each face, which is illuminated by rapid intermittent flashes.

FLASHING TRAFFIC SIGNAL - A traffic control signal used as a flashing beacon.

FLOATING CAR - An automobile driven in the traffic flow at the average speed of the surrounding vehicles.

FLOW DIAGRAM - The graphical representation of the traffic volumes on a road or street network or section thereof, showing by means of bands the relative volumes using each section of roadway during a given period of time, usually 1 hour.

H

HIGH FREQUENCY ACCIDENT LOCATION - A specific location where a large number of traffic accidents have occurred.

I

INTERSECTION APPROACH - That portion of an intersection leg which is used by traffic approaching the intersection.

L

LATERAL CLEARANCE - The distance between the edge of pavement and any lateral obstruction.

LATERAL OBSTRUCTION - Any fixed object located adjacent to the traveled way which reduces the transverse dimensions of the roadway.

LEFT TURN LANE - A lane within the normal surfaced width reserved for left turning vehicles.

M

MANUAL TRAFFIC CONTROL - The use of-hand signals or manually operated devices by traffic control personnel to control traffic.

MANUAL COUNTER - A tallying device which is operated by hand.

MASS TRANSPORTATION - Movement of large groups of persons.

MULTIAXLE TRUCK - A truck which has more than two axles.

O

OCCUPANCY RATIO -The average number-of occupants per vehicle (including the driver).

ODOMETER -A device on a vehicle for measuring the distance traveled, usually as a cumulative total, but sometimes also for individual trips, with an indicator on the instrument panel where it is usually combined with a speedometer indicator, or in the hub of a wheel in some trucks.

OFF-PEAK PERIOD - That portion of the day in which traffic volumes are relatively light.

OFFSET LANES - Additional lanes used for traffic which is heavier in one direction. Also known as unbalanced lanes.

OFF-STREET PARKING - Lots and garages intended for parking entirely off streets and alleys. street and alleys (may be angle or parallel parking) for parking of vehicles.

ORIGIN DESTINATION STUDIES - A study of the origins and destinations of trips of vehicles and passengers. Usually included in the study are all trips within, or passing through, into or out of a selected area.

OVERALL SPEED - The total distance traversed divided by the travel time. Usually expressed in miles per hour and includes all delays.

OVERALL TIME - The time of travel, including stops and delays except those off the traveled way.

P

PARALLEL PARKING - Parking where the longitudinal axis of vehicles are parallel to alignment of the roadway so that the vehicles are facing in the same direction as the movement of adjacent vehicular traffic.

PARKING DURATION - Length of time a vehicle is parked.

PASSENGER VEHICLE - A free-wheeled, self-propelled vehicle designed for the transportation of persons but limited in seating capacity to not more than seven passengers, not including the driver. It includes taxicabs, limousines, and station wagons, but does not include motorcycles.
(In capacity studies, also includes light reconnaissance vehicles, and pickup trucks.)

PASSENGER (TRANSIT) VOLUME - The total number of public transit occupants being transported in a period of time.

PEAK PERIOD - That portion of the day in which maximum traffic volumes are experienced.

PEDESTRIAN - Any person afoot. For purpose of accident classification, this will be interpreted to include any person riding in or upon a device moved or designed for movement by human power or the force of gravity, except bicycles, including stilts, skates, skis, sleds, toy wagons, and scooters.

PERCENT OF GRADE - The slope in the longitudinal direction of the pavement expressed in percent which is the number of units of change in elevation per 100 units of horizontal distance.

PERCENT OF GREEN TIME - The percentage of green time allotted to the direction of travel being studies.

PROPERTY DAMAGE - Damage to property as a result of a motor vehicle accident that may be a basis of a claim for compensation. Does not include compensation for loss of life or for personal injuries.

PUBLIC HIGHWAYS- The entire width between property lines, or boundary lines, of every way or place of which any part is open to use of the public for purposes of vehicular traffic as a matter of right or custom.

PUBLIC TRANSIT - The public passenger carryi ng service afforded by vehicles following regular routes and making specified stops.

R

REFLECTORIZE - The application of some material to traffic control devices or hazards which will return to the eyes of the road user some portion of the light from his vehicle headlights, thereby producing a brightness which attracts attention.

REGULATORY DEVICE - A device used to indicate the required method of traffic movement or use of the public traffic way.

REGULATORY SIGN - A sign used to indicate the required method of traffic movement or use of the traffic way.

RIGHT TURN LANE - A lane within the normal surfaced width reserved for right turning vehicles.

ROADWAY - That portion of a traffic way including shoulders, improved, designed, or ordinarily used for vehicle traffic.

S

SEPARATE TURNING LANE - Added traffic lane which is separated from the intersection area by an island or unpaved area. It may be wide enough for one or two line operation

SHOULDER - The portion of the roadway contiguous with the traveled way for accommodation of stopped vehicles, for emergency use, and for lateral support of base and surface courses.

SIGHT DISTANCES - The length of roadway visible to the driver of a passenger vehicle at any given point on the roadway when the view is unobstructed by traffic.

SIGNAL CYCLE - The total time required for one complete sequence of the intervals of a traffic signal.

SIGNAL CONTROLLER - A complete electrical mechanism for controlling the operation of traffic control signals, including the timer and all necessary auxiliary apparatus mounted in a cabinet.

SIGNAL FACE - That part of a signal head provided for controlling traffic from a single direction.

SIGNAL HEAD - An assembly containing one or more signal faces that may be designated accordingly as one-way, two-way, multi-way.

SIGNAL PHASE - A part of the total time cycle allocated to movements receiving the right-of-way or to any combination ments receiving the right-of-way simultaneously during one

SIMPLE INTERSECTION - An intersection of two traffic ways, approaches.

SPEED - The rate of movement of a vehicle, generally expressed in miles per hour.

STOPPING SIGHT DISTANCE --The distance required by a drive of a vehicle, given speed, to bring vehicle to a stop after and object becomes visible.

STREET WIDTH - The width of the paved or traveled portion of the roadway.

T

THROUGH MOVEMENT - (See THROUGH TRAFFIC)

THROUGH STREET - A street on which traffic is given the right-of-way so that vehicles entering or crossing the street must yield the right-of-way.

THROUGH TRAFFIC - Traffic proceeding through a military installation or portion not originating in or destined to that military installation or portion thereof.

TIME CYCLE - (See SIGNAL CYCLE)

TRAFFIC - Pedestrians, ridden or herded animals, vehicles, street cars, and other conveyances, either singly or together, while using any street for purposes of travel.

TRAFFIC ACCIDENT - Any accident involving a motor vehicle in motion that results in death, injury, or property damage.

TRAFFIC ACTUATED CONTROLLER- An automatic controller for supervising the operation of traffic control signals in accordance with the immediate and varying demands of traffic as registered with the-controller by means of detectors.

TRAFFIC CONTROL - All measures except those of a structural kind that serve to control and guide traffic and to promote road safety.

TRAFFIC CONTROL DEVICE - A Traffic control device is any sign, signal, marking, or device placed or erected for the purpose of regulating, warning, or guiding traffic.

TRAFFIC DEMAND - The volume of traffic desiring to use a particular route or facility.

TRAFFIC ENGINEERING - That phase of engineering that deals with the planning and geometric design of streets, highways, and abutting lands, and with traffic operations thereon, as their use is related to the safe, convenient, and economic transportation of persons and goods.

TRAFFIC FLOW - The movement of vehicles on a roadway.

TRAFFIC FLOW PATTERN - The distribution of traffic volumes on a street or highway network~

TRAFFIC GENERATOR - A traffic producing area such as a post exchange, parking lot, or administrative center.

TRAFFIC SIGNAL INTERVAL - Anyone of the several divisions of the total time cycle during which signal indications do not change.

TRAFFICWAY - The entire width between property lines (or other boundary lines) of every way or place of which any part is open to use of public for purposes of vehicular traffic as a matter of right or custom.

TRANSIT VEHICLE - A passenger carrying vehicle, such as a bus or streetcar which follows regular routes and makes specific stops.

TRAVEL TIME- The total elapsed time from the origin to destination of a trip.

TURNING MOVEMENT - The traffic making a designated turn at an intersection.

TWO-WAY STREETS - A street on which traffic may move in opposite directions simultaneously. It may be either divided or undivided.

TYPE OF ACCIDENT - The kind of motor vehicle accident, such as head-on, right-angle, etc.

TYPE OF SURFACE - The class of surface such as concrete, asphalt, gravel, etc.

U

UNINTERRRUPTED FLOW - The flow of-vehicles under ideal conditions resulting in unrestricted movement.

V

VEHICLE - Every device in, upon, or by which any person or property is or may be transported or drawn upon a highway, except those devices moved by human power or used exclusively upon stationary rails or tracks.

VEHICULE OCCUPANCY - The average number of occupants per automobile, including the driver.

VOLUME - The number of vehicles passing a given point during a specified period of time.

W

WARNING SIGN - A sign used to indicate conditions that are actually or potentially hazardous to highway users.

WARRANT - Formally stated conditions that have been accepted as minimum requirements for justifying installation of a traffic control device or regulation.

Z

ZONE (ORIGIN-DESTINATION STUDIES) -- A division of an area established for the purpose of analyzing origin-destination studies. It may be bounded by physical barriers such as rivers and highways, or may be the location of individual work organizations that have duty stations in relatively close proximity.

ELECTRICAL TERMS AND FORMULAS

CONTENTS

	Page
TERMS	1
Agonic ...... Dielectric	1
Diode ...... Lead	2
Line of Force ...... Resistor	3
Retentivity ...... Wattmeter	4
FORMULAS	4
Ohm's Law for D-C Circuits	4
Resistors in Series	4
Resistors in Parallel	4
R-L Circuit Time Constant	5
R-C Circuit Time Constant	5
Comparison of Units in Electric and Magnetic Circuits	5
Capacitors in Series	5
Capacitors in Parallel	5
Capacitive Reactance	5
Impedance in an R-C Circuit (Series)	5
Inductors in Series	5
Inductors in Parallel	5
Inductive Reactance	5
Q of a Coil	5
Impedance of an R-L Circuit (Series)	5
Impedance with R, C, and L in Series	5
Parallel Circuit Impedance	5
Sine-Wave Voltage Relationships	5
Power in A-C Circuit	6
Transformers	6
Three-Phase Voltage and Current Relationships	6
GREEK ALPHABET	7
Alpha ...... Omega	7
COMMON ABBREVIATIONS AND LETTER SYMBOLS	8
Alternating Current (noun) ...... Watt	8

ELECTRICAL TERMS AND FORMULAS

Terms

AGONIC.—An imaginary line of the earth's surface passing through points where the magnetic declination is 0°; that is, points where the compass points to true north.

AMMETER.—An instrument for measuring the amount of electron flow in amperes.

AMPERE.—The basic unit of electrical current.

AMPERE-TURN.—The magnetizing force produced by a current of one ampere flowing through a coil of one turn.

AMPLIDYNE.—A rotary magnetic or dynamoelectric amplifier used in servomechanism and control applications.

AMPLIFICATION.—The process of increasing the strength (current, power, or voltage) of a signal.

AMPLIFIER.—A device used to increase the signal voltage, current, or power, generally composed of a vacuum tube and associated circuit called a stage. It may contain several stages in order to obtain a desired gain.

AMPLITUDE.—The maximum instantaneous value of an alternating voltage or current, measured in either the positive or negative direction.

ARC.—A flash caused by an electric current ionizing a gas or vapor.

ARMATURE.—The rotating part of an electric motor or generator. The moving part of a relay or vibrator.

ATTENUATOR.—A network of resistors used to reduce voltage, current, or power delivered to a load.

AUTOTRANSFORMER.—A transformer in which the primary and secondary are connected together in one winding.

BATTERY.—Two or more primary or secondary cells connected together electrically. The term does not apply to a single cell.

BREAKER POINTS.—Metal contacts that open and close a circuit at timed intervals.

BRIDGE CIRCUIT.—The electrical bridge circuit is a term referring to any one of a variety of electric circuit networks, one branch of which, the "bridge" proper, connects two points of equal potential and hence carries no current when the circuit is properly adjusted or balanced.

BRUSH.—The conducting material, usually a block of carbon, bearing against the commutator or sliprings through which the current flows in or out.

BUS BAR.—A primary power distribution point connected to the main power source.

CAPACITOR.—Two electrodes or sets of electrodes in the form of plates, separated from each other by an insulating material called the dielectric.

CHOKE COIL.—A coil of low ohmic resistance and high impedance to alternating current.

CIRCUIT.—The complete path of an electric current.

CIRCUIT BREAKER.—An electromagnetic or thermal device that opens a circuit when the current in the circuit exceeds a predetermined amount. Circuit breakers can be reset.

CIRCULAR MIL.—An area equal to that of a circle with a diameter of 0.001 inch. It is used for measuring the cross section of wires.

COAXIAL CABLE.—A transmission line consisting of two conductors concentric with and insulated from each other.

COMMUTATOR.—The copper segments on the armature of a motor or generator. It is cylindrical in shape and is used to pass power into or from the brushes. It is a switching device.

CONDUCTANCE.—The ability of a material to conduct or carry an electric current. It is the reciprocal of the resistance of the material, and is expressed in mhos.

CONDUCTIVITY.—The ease with which a substance transmits electricity.

CONDUCTOR.—Any material suitable for carrying electric current.

CORE.—A magnetic material that affords an easy path for magnetic flux lines in a coil.

COUNTER E.M.F.—Counter electromotive force; an e.m.f. induced in a coil or armature that opposes the applied voltage.

CURRENT LIMITER.—A protective device similar to a fuse, usually used in high amperage circuits.

CYCLE.—One complete positive and one complete negative alternation of a current or voltage.

DIELECTRIC.—An insulator; a term that refers to the insulating material between the plates of a capacitor.

ELECTRICAL TERMS AND FORMULAS

DIODE.—Vacuum tube—a two element tube that contains a cathode and plate; semiconductor—a material of either germanium or silicon that is manufactured to allow current to flow in only one direction. Diodes are used as rectifiers and detectors.

DIRECT CURRENT.—An electric current that flows in one direction only.

EDDY CURRENT.—Induced circulating currents in a conducting material that are caused by a varying magnetic field.

EFFICIENCY.—The ratio of output power to input power, generally expressed as a percentage.

ELECTROLYTE.—A solution of a substance which is capable of conducting electricity. An electrolyte may be in the form of either a liquid or a paste.

ELECTROMAGNET.—A magnet made by passing current through a coil of wire wound on a soft iron core.

ELECTROMOTIVE FORCE (e.m.f.).—The force that produces an electric current in a circuit.

ELECTRON.—A negatively charged particle of matter.

ENERGY.—The ability or capacity to do work.

FARAD.—The unit of capacitance.

FEEDBACK.—A transfer of energy from the output circuit of a device back to its input.

FIELD.—The space containing electric or magnetic lines of force.

FIELD WINDING.—The coil used to provide the magnetizing force in motors and generators.

FLUX FIELD.—All electric or magnetic lines of force in a given region.

FREE ELECTRONS.—Electrons which are loosely held and consequently tend to move at random among the atoms of the material.

FREQUENCY.—The number of complete cycles per second existing in any form of wave motion; such as the number of cycles per second of an alternating current.

FULL-WAVE RECTIFIER CIRCUIT.—A circuit which utilizes both the positive and the negative alternations of an alternating current to produce a direct current.

FUSE.—A protective device inserted in series with a circuit. It contains a metal that will melt or break when current is increased beyond a specific value for a definite period of time.

GAIN.—The ratio of the output power, voltage, or current to the input power, voltage, or current, respectively.

GALVANOMETER.—An instrument used to measure small d-c currents.

GENERATOR.—A machine that converts mechanical energy into electrical energy.

GROUND.—A metallic connection with the earth to establish ground potential. Also, a common return to a point of zero potential. The chassis of a receiver or a transmitter is sometimes the common return, and therefore the ground of the unit.

HENRY.—The basic unit of inductance.

HORSEPOWER.—The English unit of power, equal to work done at the rate of 550 foot-pounds per second. Equal to 746 watts of electrical power.

HYSTERESIS.—A lagging of the magnetic flux in a magnetic material behind the magnetizing force which is producing it.

IMPEDANCE.—The total opposition offered to the flow of an alternating current. It may consist of any combination of resistance, inductive reactance, and capacitive reactance.

INDUCTANCE.—The property of a circuit which tends to oppose a change in the existing current.

INDUCTION.—The act or process of producing voltage by the relative motion of a magnetic field across a conductor.

INDUCTIVE REACTANCE.—The opposition to the flow of alternating or pulsating current caused by the inductance of a circuit. It is measured in ohms.

INPHASE.—Applied to the condition that exists when two waves of the same frequency pass through their maximum and minimum values of like polarity at the same instant.

INVERSELY.—Inverted or reversed in position or relationship.

ISOGONIC LINE.—An imaginary line drawn through points on the earth's surface where the magnetic deviation is equal.

JOULE.—A unit of energy or work. A joule of energy is liberated by one ampere flowing for one second through a resistance of one ohm.

KILO.—A prefix meaning 1,000.

LAG.—The amount one wave is behind another in time; expressed in electrical degrees.

LAMINATED CORE.—A core built up from thin sheets of metal and used in transformers and relays.

LEAD.—The opposite of LAG. Also, a wire or connection.

ELECTRICAL TERMS AND FORMULAS

LINE OF FORCE.—A line in an electric or magnetic field that shows the direction of the force.

LOAD.—The power that is being delivered by any power producing device. The equipment that uses the power from the power producing device.

MAGNETIC AMPLIFIER.—A saturable reactor type device that is used in a circuit to amplify or control.

MAGNETIC CIRCUIT.—The complete path of magnetic lines of force.

MAGNETIC FIELD.—The space in which a magnetic force exists.

MAGNETIC FLUX.—The total number of lines of force issuing from a pole of a magnet.

MAGNETIZE.—To convert a material into a magnet by causing the molecules to rearrange.

MAGNETO.—A generator which produces alternating current and has a permanent magnet as its field.

MEGGER.—A test instrument used to measure insulation resistance and other high resistances. It is a portable hand operated d-c generator used as an ohmmeter.

MEGOHM.—A million ohms.

MICRO.—A prefix meaning one-millionth.

MILLI.—A prefix meaning one-thousandth.

MILLIAMMETER.—An ammeter that measures current in thousandths of an ampere.

MOTOR-GENERATOR.—A motor and a generator with a common shaft used to convert line voltages to other voltages or frequencies.

MUTUAL INDUCTANCE.—A circuit property existing when the relative position of two inductors causes the magnetic lines of force from one to link with the turns of the other.

NEGATIVE CHARGE.—The electrical charge carried by a body which has an excess of electrons.

NEUTRON.—A particle having the weight of a proton but carrying no electric charge. It is located in the nucleus of an atom.

NUCLEUS.—The central part of an atom that is mainly comprised of protons and neutrons. It is the part of the atom that has the most mass.

NULL.—Zero.

OHM.—The unit of electrical resistance.

OHMMETER.—An instrument for directly measuring resistance in ohms.

OVERLOAD.—A load greater than the rated load of an electrical device.

PERMALLOY.—An alloy of nickel and iron having an abnormally high magnetic permeability.

PERMEABILITY.—A measure of the ease with which magnetic lines of force can flow through a material as compared to air.

PHASE DIFFERENCE.—The time in electrical degrees by which one wave leads or lags another.

POLARITY.—The character of having magnetic poles, or electric charges.

POLE.—The section of a magnet where the flux lines are concentrated; also where they enter and leave the magnet. An electrode of a battery.

POLYPHASE.—A circuit that utilizes more than one phase of alternating current.

POSITIVE CHARGE.—The electrical charge carried by a body which has become deficient in electrons.

POTENTIAL.—The amount of charge held by a body as compared to another point or body. Usually measured in volts.

POTENTIOMETER.—A variable voltage divider; a resistor which has a variable contact arm so that any portion of the potential applied between its ends may be selected.

POWER.—The rate of doing work or the rate of expending energy. The unit of electrical power is the watt.

POWER FACTOR.—The ratio of the actual power of an alternating or pulsating current, as measured by a wattmeter, to the apparent power, as indicated by ammeter and voltmeter readings. The power factor of an inductor, capacitor, or insulator is an expression of their losses.

PRIME MOVER.—The source of mechanical power used to drive the rotor of a generator.

PROTON.—A positively charged particle in the nucleus of an atom.

RATIO.—The value obtained by dividing one number by another, indicating their relative proportions.

REACTANCE.—The opposition offered to the flow of an alternating current by the inductance, capacitance, or both, in any circuit.

RECTIFIERS.—Devices used to change alternating current to unidirectional current. These may be vacuum tubes, semiconductors such as germanium and silicon, and dry-disk rectifiers such as selenium and copper-oxide.

RELAY.—An electromechanical switching device that can be used as a remote control.

RELUCTANCE.—A measure of the opposition that a material offers to magnetic lines of force.

RESISTANCE.—The opposition to the flow of current caused by the nature and physical dimensions of a conductor.

RESISTOR.—A circuit element whose chief characteristic is resistance; used to oppose the flow of current.

ELECTRICAL TERMS AND FORMULAS

RETENTIVITY.—The measure of the ability of a material to hold its magnetism.

RHEOSTAT.—A variable resistor.

SATURABLE REACTOR.—A control device that uses a small d-c current to control a large a-c current by controlling core flux density.

SATURATION.—The condition existing in any circuit when an increase in the driving signal produces no further change in the resultant effect.

SELF-INDUCTION.—The process by which a circuit induces an e.m.f. into itself by its own magnetic field.

SERIES-WOUND.—A motor or generator in which the armature is wired in series with the field winding.

SERVO.—A device used to convert a small movement into one of greater movement or force.

SERVOMECHANISM.—A closed-loop system that produces a force to position an object in accordance with the information that originates at the input.

SOLENOID.—An electromagnetic coil that contains a movable plunger.

SPACE CHARGE.—The cloud of electrons existing in the space between the cathode and plate in a vacuum tube, formed by the electrons emitted from the cathode in excess of those immediately attracted to the plate.

SPECIFIC GRAVITY—The ratio between the density of a substance and that of pure water, at a given temperature.

SYNCHROSCOPE—An instrument used to indicate a difference in frequency between two a-c sources.

SYNCHRO SYSTEM.—An electrical system that gives remote indications or control by means of self-synchronizing motors.

TACHOMETER.—An instrument for indicating revolutions per minute.

TERTIARY WINDING.—A third winding on a transformer or magnetic amplifier that is used as a second control winding.

THERMISTOR.—A resistor that is used to compensate for temperature variations in a circuit.

THERMOCOUPLE.—A junction of two dissimilar metals that produces a voltage when heated.

TORQUE.—The turning effort or twist which a shaft sustains when transmitting power.

TRANSFORMER.—A device composed of two or more coils, linked by magnetic lines of force, used to transfer energy from one circuit to another.

TRANSMISSION LINES.—Any conductor or system of conductors used to carry electrical energy from its source to a load.

VARS.—Abbreviation for volt-ampere, reactive.

VECTOR.—A line used to represent both direction and magnitude.

VOLT.—The unit of electrical potential.

VOLTMETER.—An instrument designed to measure a difference in electrical potential, in volts.

WATT.—The unit of electrical power.

WATTMETER.—An instrument for measuring electrical power in watts.

Formulas

Ohm's Law for d-c Circuits

$$I = \frac{E}{R} = \frac{P}{E} = \sqrt{\frac{P}{R}}$$

$$R = \frac{E}{I} = \frac{P}{I^2} = \frac{E^2}{P}$$

$$E = IR = \frac{P}{I} = \sqrt{PR}$$

$$P = EI = \frac{E^2}{R} = I^2 R$$

Resistors in Series

$$R_T = R_1 + R_2 \ldots$$

Resistors in Parallel
Two resistors

$$R_T = \frac{R_1 R_2}{R_1 + R_2}$$

More than two

$$\frac{1}{R_T} = \frac{1}{R_1} + \frac{1}{R_2} + \frac{1}{R_3}$$

ELECTRICAL TERMS AND FORMULAS

R-L Circuit Time Constant equals

$$\frac{L \text{ (in henrys)}}{R \text{ (in ohms)}} = t \text{ (in seconds), or}$$

$$\frac{L \text{ (in microhenrys)}}{R \text{ (in ohms)}} = t \text{ (in microseconds)}$$

R-C Circuit Time Constant equals
R (ohms) × C (farads) = t (seconds)
R (megohms) × C (microfarads) = t (seconds)
R (ohms) × C (microfarads) = t (microseconds)
R (megohms) × C (micromicrofrads = t (microseconds)

Comparison of Units in Electric and Magnetic Circuits.

	Electric circuit	Magnetic circuit
Force	Volt, E or e.m.f.	Gilberts, F, or m.m.f.
Flow	Ampere, I	Flux, Φ, in maxwells
Opposition	Ohms, R	Reluctance, R
Law	Ohm's law, $I = \frac{E}{R}$	Rowland's law $\Phi = \frac{F}{R}$
Intensity of force	Volts per cm. of length	$H = \frac{1.257 IN}{L}$, gilberts per centimeter of length
Density	Current density— for example, amperes per cm^2.	Flux density—for example, lines per cm^2., or gausses

Capacitors in Series
Two capacitors

$$C_T = \frac{C_1 C_2}{C_1 + C_2}$$

More than two

$$\frac{1}{C_T} = \frac{1}{C_1} + \frac{1}{C_2} + \frac{1}{C_3}...$$

Capacitors in Parallel

$$C_T = C_1 + C_2 ...$$

Capacitive Reactance

$$X_c = \frac{1}{2\pi f C}$$

Impedance in an R-C Circuit (Series)

$$Z = \sqrt{R^2 + X_c^2}$$

Inductors in Series

$$L_T = L_1 + L_2 ... \text{(No coupling between coils)}$$

Inductors in Parallel
Two inductors

$$L_T = \frac{L_1 L_2}{L_1 + L_2} \text{ (No coupling between coils)}$$

More than two

$$\frac{1}{L_T} = \frac{1}{L_1} + \frac{1}{L_2} + \frac{1}{L_3} ... \text{ (No coupling between coils)}$$

Inductive Reactance

$$X_L = 2\pi f L$$

Q of a Coil

$$Q = \frac{X_L}{R}$$

Impedance of an R-L Circuit (series)

$$Z = \sqrt{R^2 + X_L^2}$$

Impedance with R, C, and L in Series

$$Z = \sqrt{R^2 + (X_L - X_C)^2}$$

Parallel Circuit Impedance

$$Z = \frac{Z_1 Z_2}{Z_1 + Z_2}$$

Sine-Wave Voltage Relationships
Average value

$$E_{ave} = \frac{2}{\pi} \times E_{max} = 0.637 E_{max}$$

ELECTRICAL TERMS AND FORMULAS

Effective or r.m.s. value

$$E_{eff} = \frac{E_{max}}{\sqrt{2}} = \frac{E_{max}}{1.414} = 0.707 E_{max} = 1.11 E_{ave}$$

Maximum value

$$E_{max} = \sqrt{2} E_{eff} = 1.414 E_{eff} = 1.57 E_{ave}$$

Voltage in an a-c circuit

$$E = IZ = \frac{P}{I \times P.F.}$$

Current in an a-c circuit

$$I = \frac{E}{Z} = \frac{P}{E \times P.F.}$$

Power in A-C Circuit
Apparent power = EI
True power

$$P = EI \cos\theta = EI \times P.F.$$

Power factor

$$P.F. = \frac{P}{EI} = \cos\theta$$

$$\cos\theta = \frac{\text{true power}}{\text{apparent power}}$$

Transformers
Voltage relationship

$$\frac{E}{E} = \frac{N}{N} \text{ or } E = E \times \frac{N}{N}$$

Current relationship

$$\frac{I_p}{I_s} = \frac{N_s}{N_p}$$

Induced voltage

$$E_{eff} = 4.44 \, BAfN \, 10^{-8}$$

Turns ratio equals

$$\frac{N_p}{N_s} = \sqrt{\frac{Z_p}{Z_s}}$$

Secondary current

$$I_s = I_p \frac{N_p}{N_s}$$

Secondary voltage

$$E_s = E_p \frac{N_s}{N_p}$$

Three Phase Voltage and Current Relationships
With wye connected windings

$$E_{line} = 1.732 E_{coil} = \sqrt{3} E_{coil}$$

$$I_{line} = I_{coil}$$

With delta connected windings

$$E_{line} = E_{coil}$$

$$I_{line} = 1.732 I_{coil}$$

With wye or delta connected winding

$$P_{coil} = E_{coil} I_{coil}$$

$$P_t = 3 P_{coil}$$

$$P_t = 1.732 E_{line} I_{line}$$

(To convert to true power multiply by $\cos\theta$)

Synchronous Speed of Motor

$$r.p.m. = \frac{120 \times \text{frequency}}{\text{number of poles}}$$

GREEK ALPHABET

Name	Capital	Lower Case	Designates
Alpha	A	α	Angles.
Beta	B	β	Angles, flux density.
Gamma	Γ	γ	Conductivity.
Delta	Δ	δ	Variation of a quantity, increment.
Epsilon	E	ϵ	Base of natural logarithms (2.71828).
Zeta	Z	ζ	Impedance, coefficients, coordinates.
Eta	H	η	Hysteresis coefficient, efficiency, magnetizing force.
Theta	Θ	θ	Phase angle.
Iota	I	ι	
Kappa	K	κ	Dielectric constant, coupling coefficient, susceptibility.
Lambda	Λ	λ	Wavelength.
Mu	M	μ	Permeability, micro, amplification factor.
Nu	N	ν	Reluctivity.
Xi	Ξ	ξ	
Omicron	O	o	
Pi	Π	π	3.1416
Rho	P	ρ	Resistivity.
Sigma	Σ	σ	
Tau	T	τ	Time constant, time-phase displacement.
Upsilon	Υ	υ	
Phi	Φ	φ	Angles, magnetic flux.
Chi	X	χ	
Psi	Ψ	ψ	Dielectric flux, phase difference.
Omega	Ω	ω	Ohms (capital), angular velocity ($2\pi f$).

COMMON ABBREVIATIONS AND LETTER SYMBOLS

Term	Abbreviation or Symbol
alternating current (noun)	a.c.
alternating-current (adj.)	a-c
ampere	a.
area	A
audiofrequency (noun)	AF
audiofrequency (adj.)	A-F
capacitance	C
capacitive reactance	X_C
centimeter	cm.
conductance	G
coulomb	Q
counterelectromotive force	c.e.m.f.
current (d-c or r.m.s. value)	I
current (instantaneous value)	i
cycles per second	c.p.s.
dielectric constant	K, k
difference in potential (d-c or r.m.s. value)	E
difference in potential (instantaneous value)	e
direct current (noun)	d.c.
direct-current (adj.)	d-c
electromotive force	e.m.f.
frequency	f
henry	h.
horsepower	hp.
impedance	Z
inductance	L
inductive reactance	X_L
kilovolt	kv.
kilovolt-ampere	kv.-a.
kilowatt	kw.
kilowatt-hour	kw.-hr.
magnetic field intensity	H
magnetomotive force	m.m.f.
megohm	M
microampere	μa.
microfarad	μf.
microhenry	μh.
micromicrofarad	$\mu\mu$f.
microvolt	μv.
milliampere	ma.
millihenry	mh.
milliwatt	mw.
mutual inductance	M
power	P
resistance	R
revolutions per minute	r.p.m.
root mean square	r.m.s.
time	t
torque	T
volt	v.
watt	w.